D1394486

THE BBC *AND*
PUBLIC SERVICE
BROADCASTING

Images
of culture

The series will publish work from the John Logie
Baird Centre for Research in Television and Film.
The Centre is committed to the analysis and
understanding of the history of the institutions of
cinema and television and to the analysis of the
aesthetic forms which these institutions have
produced. While drawing on contemporary critical
theory and its development of semiotics,
psychoanalysis, and Marxism, the work of the
Centre is committed to specific analyses and to a
dialogue with practitioners. A commitment to a
positive discrimination within popular culture and
to an engagement with the politics of the media will
be a feature of work in this series.

also in this series

HIGH THEORY /
LOW CULTURE
ed. COLIN MACCABE

COLIN MACCABE
OLIVIA STEWART *editors*

THE BBC *AND* PUBLIC SERVICE BROADCASTING

MANCHESTER
UNIVERSITY PRESS

Published by MANCHESTER UNIVERSITY PRESS,
Oxford Road, Manchester, M13 9PL, UK

The BBC and public service broadcasting
    —(Images of culture) 1. Radio programs, Public service
    2. Television programs, Public service   3. Broadcasting
    I. MacCabe, Colin   II. Stewart, Olivia   III. Series
    384.54'53   HE8689.7.P8

ISBN 0-7190-1964-8
ISBN 0-7190-1965-6 *paperback*

TYPESET IN GALLIARD BY KOINONIA LTD, MANCHESTER

Printed in Great Britain
BY THE ALDEN PRESS, OXFORD

Contents

NOTES ON CONTRIBUTORS

Colin MacCabe is Head of the Production Division of the British Film Institute and visiting Professor at the Universities of Pittsburgh and Strathclyde.

Olivia Stewart was until recently Research Fellow at the Broadcasting Research Unit and now works for the British Film Institute Production Division.

John Caughie is Lecturer in Film and Television Studies at the University of Glasgow and Director of the John Logie Baird Centre for Research in Television and Film.

David Elstein was Managing Director of Primetime Television at the time of the seminar. In April 1986 he became Director of Programmes of Thames Television.

Jeremy Isaacs is Chief Executive of Channel 4 Television.

Charles Jonscher is Managing Director of Communications Studies and Planning International and also lectures at the Massachusetts Institute of Technology.

Krishan Kumar is a Reader in Sociology at the University of Kent.

Brenda Maddox is the author of *Beyond Babel: New Directions in Communications,* and of other books.

William Maley is a PhD student at Jesus College, Cambridge.

Margaret Matheson is Director of Production of Zenith Productions Ltd.

Janet Morgan is a consultant and writer on political and administrative history and new technologies. She is currently Special Adviser to the Director General of the BBC.

Anthony Smith is Director of the British Film Institute.

PREFACE

The first fifty years of broadcasting in Britain saw widespread agreement as to the general aims of broadcasting and the way in which those aims are defined by the State. The single phrase that is used to cover this historic agreement is 'public service broadcasting'. In recent years, however, this widespread agreement has broken down and with that breakdown the phrase 'public service broadcasting' has become more and more of a token gesture to some notional agreement rather than a description with any definite content.

It was in an attempt to understand the current disagreements and to investigate the possibilities of new and serious content to the notion of public service broadcasting that the Logie Baird Centre organised its annual seminar in 1985. The government's announcement of the Peacock Committee's investigation into the funding of the BBC means that when the seminar convened the subject had become intensely topical. This topicality should not, however, obscure the long-term cultural and economic problems which the seminar addressed and to which any single government report will only be incidental.

Public service broadcasting has traditionally based its arguments on questions of cultural value. The aim has always been to provide a mix of programming by which audiences may be educated as well as entertained. These aesthetic and cultural arguments have always assumed technologies which ensure that there can be no direct relationship between viewers and broadcasters. Audiences can pay for their programmes through forms of taxation or through increased costs of goods advertised but they have not been able to pay directly for programmes. An additional assumption has been that the broadcasters have complete control over both scheduling and content of the home television screen.

Recent technological advances have transformed this situation. The video cassette recorder has allowed every viewer to be his/her own scheduler and the immense growth of video hire has allowed many viewers to become their own programmers as well. And the changes that are to come will be as significant. In particular, as Charles Jonscher describes in Chapter 5, there will soon be viable methods of direct subscription for television.

It is this context which informs the papers gathered together here. Despite their diversity of approach they share a common desire to provide the terms to understand the relation between individual viewer, cultural production and political institutions. Questions about the history of the concept of public service broadcasting and the concomitant history of the BBC and the other broadcasting organisations run into questions about future methods of funding, both in terms of national broadcasting systems and the financing of individual productions. The section on co-production makes clear to what extent television is now part of the international diversification of both economics and culture which leave our national political institutions looking more and more outmoded and ineffective. Indeed, in many ways the underlying unity of the following chapters might be found in the differing perspectives that they offer on the possibilities and potentialities of our national culture. Questions of public service broadcasting are not the arcane preserve of professional broadcasters. They are central to the kind of society that we are and that we are likely to become. This volume will have served its purpose if it makes clear the immense social consequences of technical questions of funding and aesthetic questions of quality.

The seminar would not have been possible without the support and encouragement of the Advisory Board and Stephen Hearst in particular. Thanks are due to the BBC, Channel 4, Scottish Television, the Acton Society and the Broadcasting Research Unit, all of whom made contributions to the cost of the seminar.

Colin MacCabe

chapter 1 ANTHONY SMITH

Licences and liberty:
public service broadcasting
in Britain

Anyone who has engaged professionally in broadcasting will
recognise how it obliges one constantly to take positions,
explicitly or implicitly, on a great range of sciences and
specialisations. That is in the nature of the whole heterogeneous business. Once when Reith was interviewing a
trembling graduate applying for a job he enquired whether
the interviewee was proficient in music. 'No,' was the reply.
Then whether he was proficient in electricity. 'No,' was the
reply again. 'Then you are applying for the wrong job,' said
Reith, 'for those are the two things with which the BBC is
principally concerned. Music and Electricity.' In broadcasting those who at one level are simply making themselves
responsible for a communication medium automatically find
themselves taking pre-emptive and far-reaching judgements
not only about music and electricity, but also about politics,
economics, psychology, defence, industry, whatever the subject of their programme. They exert a patronage over vast
territories in which they cannot, in the nature of things, claim
any proficiency. The judgements of producers, directors,
researchers, represent a source of unelective social power and
the whole endless debate about broadcasting since the 1920s
has, at root, been about the process of legitimising, demo-
cratising, harnessing, mitigating, denying or undermining
that power. Only relatively recently has the focus of the

debate been economics. Most of the endless series of official enquiries have concerned themselves with structures and public accountability, with essentially political issues.

It is temporarily fashionable in Britain to analyse everything in terms of money, as if income and expenditure represented the reality of things rather than a measure of them. So let me start with the vogue and begin by saying something about the financial framework of broadcasting in Britain, for it does not fit easily into normal methods of economic analysis.

In radio and television no transaction takes place between supplier and market. It is a system for the gratuitous distribution of a highly differentiated series of goods and the decisions which shape the system and those goods have always been and always will be far more political than economic in nature. The right to disseminate information and entertainment through the ether is a privilege granted by authority to a company or institution. There may not exist competition among a group of suppliers; there may not be the sale of advertising time as a method of revenue. The primary market of viewers and listeners will, nonetheless, receive the product without a direct transaction. Broadcasting is similar to the supplying of water, similar to the State education system, to defence, in that it exists first by political decision, and a system of revenue is built around it. The licence to operate is granted ultimately by the powers that be within a society; they decide how the service concerned is to be paid for, and on what conditions its managers will have to work.

At the end of many decades of slow building of broadcasting institutions, the British system has evolved a nexus of three interlocking monopolies, supervised by two quasi-governmental boards. The three monopolies are firstly the licence fee, paid by viewers wholly to the BBC, with its spectrum of radio stations and two television channels; secondly, the monopoly of television advertising time on two channels granted by the IBA to over a dozen commercial franchises; thirdly, the monopoly of the special levy paid by those companies to Channel 4. Nowhere in our system does a group of entrepreneurs compete against another group of entrepreneurs for a single source of revenue. That is not an accident. It is the deliberate result of all the thinking and planning of the last sixty years.

Within the BBC, radio and television compete for a share of the licence fee, news competes against drama for resources, current affairs against light entertainment, production against administration. ITV companies compete against the BBC for audiences; they compete in international market places for programmes, and also to sell programmes. Nonetheless, ITV's unbreached monopoly of advertising time is basically unaffected by anything other than its concomitant obligations to the public authority, the IBA, which dishes out and withdraws its licences to operate. The precise share-out of the available audience between BBC and ITV also does not affect the revenue of either party. Advertisers do not mind whether ITV has 45 or 50 per cent of the audience, although they might if there were a competing outlet for their advertising. Channel 4's audience similarly has no influence upon its revenue, which is decided year by year by the IBA. Only in the very longest of runs could alterations in audience size affect the revenue of any channel, and the alterations would have to be dramatic, so dramatic that they would have been remedied by administrative changes before any financial cataclysm could intervene. Of course, there are many factors which can influence the income of ITV, such as the general state of the economy, the levels of consumer spending, but the day-to-day audience of programmes is not among them.

In Britain the instinct for monopoly runs very deep, certainly within the whole culture of broadcasting. Even in industries where the process of privatisation or de-regulation has been recently imposed, it is interesting to see how patterns of rationalisation and corporate takeover help to eliminate the steady day-by-day slogging out between company and company. Perhaps this will change, but in broadcasting we still have our familiar atavistic system of carefully demarcated monopolies.

From the moment when Reith, founder of the BBC, in a characteristically Hobbesian phrase, declared that 'the brute force of monopoly' had created the great diversity of the BBC's programmes, the attention of broadcasting administrators has been unswervingly concentrated upon the belief that competition for resources would narrow and corrode the programmes both of radio and television. Any proposal for introducing a measure of financial competition has always been turned down. We do not even have in Britain competitive programme journals. Competition for audiences has, however, been extremely, indeed somewhat bafflingly, fierce, especially since the introduction of ITV in the 1950s, but possibly earlier since there was a certain amount of concealed competition between the BBC in the 1930s and the overseas commercial radio stations of Normandie and Luxembourg.

Much of the *talk* about broadcasting, in Parliament and the Press, before special committees of investigation, has centred on the issue of pluralism, the breaking of monopoly. The whole drive for commercial television in the 1950s was camouflaged as a campaign to break the monopoly of the BBC. What was done, however, in the funding of ITV, of BBC2 and now of Channel 4, was to bring about an extension and duplication of monopoly, disguised as economic pluralism.

The explanation of our disingenuous approach to broadcasting structure lies surely in a deep-bred fear of the cultural and social results of out-and-out competition between channels. If each broadcasting outlet fought for its life when it fought for its audience, then, it has always been believed, the diversity would go out of the system as broadcasting managers chose material which was known to be able to command large audiences. Competition would bring about a breakdown in the service of minorities. It would homogenise the rival channels. This belief has been maintained for half a century and the Annan Committee, a decade ago, upheld the dictum that a competing channel should never draw its income from the same source as its direct rival. The Annan Committee was right. There is no broadcasting system in the world today which does anything but underline the validity of this view.

There are those today who believe that a little experiment in *financial* pluralism would now be timely. They are, in my view, wrong in their failure to understand the nature of the licence fee, and its implications for the institution which is built upon it, and therefore of the other institutions also which have been built as a response to it.

The licence fee is a very simple device for funding a non-transactional medium. Television is not the same as cable, nor as pay television, nor as video or satellite, which are all by their nature transactional media and the kinds of material they can offer – the culture of those media, if you like – bear witness to their different economic nature. The audiences can purchase their wares one at a time. The licence fee is a price, adjudged from time to time by government as ultimate enabler of the whole system, for a total service within which a large element of financial redistribution is entailed. Large sums are spent on certain kinds of programmes, small sums on others, without reference to respective audience sizes. Popularity of programmes is not linked, in either direction, with the cost of individual transmissions. Furthermore, the costs of the transmission system itself, that is the engineering of the television channel, are equalised, via the licence fee system, between urban areas, where transmission costs are a few pence per head, and rural and mountainous areas where the cost can be many pounds per head or even tens of pounds per head. The licence fee also conveniently submerges capital and revenue into a single annual payment. It is a poll-tax of

The point

a kind and regressive in a way, since rich and poor pay the same sum, but it is also very highly redistributive by its nature. If you examine a truly commercial system like that of the USA, you will be struck, as everyone is, by the large number of channels in the inexpensive urban area, by the predictability and sameness of the programmes of rivals. But if you penetrate to the hinterland, you will be struck also by the very small numbers of channels which reach a very large proportion of the population – it took decades for television even to reach certain parts of the country. That is because it is not deemed economic to provide local transmitters and local stations in places without large or prosperous populations.

If this poll-tax of a licence fee is mixed with advertising, as it is in several European countries, then the faults rather than the benefits of both methods of revenue-raising are emphasised automatically. Advertising will tend to diminish the redistributive elements, or act as a disincentive, while the licence fee will appear increasingly to be unfairly subsidising a commercial operation. Why should the licence fee remain the property of one organisation, in other words, if advertising fails to remain the exclusive property of the another?

There exist other important and unnoticed differences between the two funding methods. The ultimate decisions about the size of the licence fee are taken, of course, by government, by politicians, after consultations with a variety of relevant persons. With advertising, the real decisions on the placement of cash are taken by people who measure audiences or who believe the results of audience measurement. These measurements have the same kind of precision as pre-election polling. Better methods are constantly being devised and tried out and complex though interesting technical arguments take place concerning the comparative reliability of methods. Happily, we have never chosen to use these systems to replace elections in the political sphere. It is one thing to sample an electorate and enquire about preferences in politics in a given week. It is quite another to sample television receivers, which may be switched on without anyone being in the room, or with people in the room who are not actually watching, who may be asleep or playing cards or listening to music on headphones. It is fortunate that in Britain the measuring of audiences has been carried out not to decide the levels of revenue for any system, but merely to satisfy curiosity and to feed institutional rivalries. In a truly competitive commercial system the measurement of audiences through crude methods of sampling is paramount; programmes, channels, whole companies even, can be swept away through the presence of unknown statistical bugs. In America vast quantities of investment in pilot programmes are regularly junked on the basis of ratings divergences well within the margins of statistical error. It is the extension of roulette into culture. The undoubted benefits of advertising are swept away when advertisers are hunted by competing channels.

There does exist a third possible way of paying for broadcasting and that is funding direct by government. Not a voguish system of finance in 1980s Britain. The danger in such a system is not so much the interference of politicians, but the operations of civil servants. The levels of accountability and the techniques for distributing, withholding and calculating direct government grants should be in themselves sufficient to deter a nation from embarking upon the direct grant. Ask Canadian broadcasters or Australian what it is like to try to run an organisation of public entertainment tied to the government's purse-strings. Treasury officials and even producers belong in different worlds, and neither can explain its actions in terms of the values of the other.

However, the real argument in favour of a unitary licence fee lies elsewhere. It lies in the potential of the nature of the unitary institution funded by it. The extraordinary flexibility of the BBC has been at times obscured by its own insistence upon secretiveness towards the public and its traditional refusal to treat itself as a truly public resource. The arrival of competition in the 1950s gave it a kind of short-sighted justification for behaving simply as one of two rival concerns. Its staff, as they became used to moving from side to side of the industry, came often, though not always, to ignore the differentness of the BBC. Trade unions, governments, management consultants, newspaper critics, advisory boards, all came to accept the idea that the BBC, the television services in particular, was destined to struggle for audiences for ever against ITV, slowly sacrificing the special ideals inherited from the funding era, as the exigencies of modern times forced compromises upon the organisation. That may be to paint too extreme a picture, but it has been a constant tendency, under constant pressures. The licence fee, however, is both symbol and infrastructure of a potentially very different relationship with audience and society from that between ITV and its audience. For the BBC must be a public resource of a special kind. It should not have to justify itself in the same terms as its rivals. It should not want to do so. It has been a simple choice on the part of its management that has resulted in its behaving since the late 1960s as but one half of a duopoly.

True, it is difficult to fit the BBC into an industrial or bureaucratic typology. It is different in kind from its rivals, and it has different, utterly different, duties. It has never been able to find the appropriate analogy for itself among other institutions, because none exists. It has chosen various role models over the years.

In the 1930s Reith came to think and feel about the BBC as if it were a kind of national church, its producers a priesthood and himself a kind of cardinal or pope, at times even perhaps a Messiah. Certainly he fulfilled his Weberian role of charismatic institutional founder and left behind a system of governance in broadcasting which remained basically intact, as Asa Briggs shows, for several decades. Like many charismatic founders of organisations he left behind essen-

tially a bureaucratic structure ministering to a set of purpo.
which had been repeatedly spelled out over a course of years.
The BBC was run partly according to the principles of
modern 1920s management which Reith had discovered
during his years in America, and which a number of successful
British firms in the private sector had also espoused – also,
some, such as the Post Office, in the public sector.

The BBC, in its era of pure monopoly, was a profession,
an industry *and* a kind of ecclesia. There simply were no
other broadcasters or managers of broadcasting in the
country. There was no other organisation competing for its
special source of funds. The institution exercised the right to
make its entire range of cultural and artistic choices. Unfor-
tunately, most students of broadcasting history have concentrated upon the BBC's political role, and have almost obsess-
ively concentrated on special issues such as the General Strike,
the treatment of Churchill, the handling of industrial and
international affairs in the 1930s. The BBC's principal role in
this society was as a mass entertainer. It lived in people's
hearts and minds because of the music it offered and the
drama and comedy. Of course, the BBC's values were clear
and it was, no doubt, as establishment-minded in its entertainment policy as in its news policy, but its points of comparison were not ITN or ILR or Channel 4 because no such
rival bodies existed. Its points of comparison were Hitler's
radio services and Mussolini's and the rapidly growing
American networks, and it worked out its relationships with
government and other heads of State, with other institutions
of the society, in silent comparison with those other nations'
broadcasting systems. Perhaps the BBC did not do much, or
not enough, to enhance democratic liberties in these islands,
but it did not really have any other system to emulate. It
concentrated its energies on entertainment; and the products
of that chief era of monopoly – the 1930s and 1940s – in
British mass media content, and here I am thinking of cinema
and the popular Press as well as radio, stand up very well to

contemporary international comparisons. What it learned institutionally at that time was how to survive within a parliamentary democracy, how to marshall silent social forces to support it, how to build a constituency as we might put it today.

In the years since the Second World War, the BBC has passed through a series of phases and has offered the world a number of quite different accounts of itself. The paternalistic values and hierarchical system of Reith gave off by the late 1940s a distinct aroma of elitism and it is from a succession of different versions of elitism that the BBC has been trying to escape ever since. With the arrival of commercial television in the 1950s, an era of contrived populism was born, the era of Mr Macmillan, of economic populism. One response to ITV, within the BBC, was the fostering of the belief in professionalism. By being a professional, the broadcaster shared something with the people who worked over in ITV. The BBC became more an employer of professionals than a church with a priesthood. In the 1960s the controllers of the BBC had also entered a phase of professionalism and the BBC, in the television service in particular, came to think of itself as a management. Lord Hill, Chairman of the BBC in the Wilson years, brought in a firm of management consultants and suddenly the familiar section heads were transmuted into a new managerial structure, with new titles and different budgets and terms of reference. The great age of managerialism was short-lived. The image did not fit. In this decade a new vogue of industrialism has emerged: in the Thatcher years, staff and management have come to see themselves as an industry. It is very fashionable today to be seen to be running an industry.

During the 1970s another half-blurred metaphor was invoked to describe and justify the ways of the Corporation, that of the foundation. For several years the sage figure of Noël Annan loomed across the whole landscape of broadcasting. The Annan Committee's deliberations became the supreme focus of all intellectual strivings. In its evidence to Annan, the BBC officials argued eloquently that the Corporation was a great 'foundation'; the phrase helped to smudge the debate over Channel 4 which has indeed emerged as a kind of foundation, providing its air time and its cash to external companies new and old who present their cases to its commissioning editors for selection.

The BBC has, of course, been and still is all of those phenomena; a kind of church, a management, a profession, an industry, a foundation, and it has been, exclusively, none of them. In an industry which offers material to a public without payment, the relationships created are different, utterly different from those which operate within a normal system of exchange. Institutions of broadcasting are simply not like companies or firms, however much one is drawn to analogise. All one can say to define the indefinable nature of the BBC is that it is a national institution.

To be a great institution it must lead. It must intervene in area after area of national life and, therefore, must build the public trust and support necessary to fulfil such a role in a democratic society. The licence fee link is not a commercial privilege of a management called the BBC, but an opportunity granted to an organisation to enhance the life of a free society through the use of a communications technology. That does not mean that the BBC is confined to one grandiose Reithian method. There has been a series of evolving organisational systems for producing programmes and the licence fee does not necessarily force the BBC into the hidebound retention of any one of them. Indeed, I believe that a new model is evolving, pioneered by Channel 4 which would help the BBC live within its ideals – perhaps live up to them more closely – and live within the licence fee.

Until recent times the argument in favour of the BBC and the licence fee has been an argument for a kind of total system. The BBC and its supporters have believed that it must, as a single organisation, operate in every field of broadcasting endeavour. When there was talk of local radio, then the BBC decided it must go into the local radio business. When there was talk of commercial breakfast television, then the BBC had to go into that business also. Satellite offers us the most egregious current example. Naturally, the licence fee has been stretched further and further in terms of its political acceptability. Now we have in Britain today a government more willing to make drastic changes than its recent predecessors, less willing to accept traditional arguments. The continuation of the BBC within the licence fee is threatened as a result directly of the BBC's need to sustain the great variety of existing services it has chosen to develop, at the quality which the audience has come to expect, at a time when commercial rivals are in a position to pay higher wages to their staff. A large family of chickens have come home to roost. They need never have been hatched.

We are evolving at this end of the century a broadcasting abundant in channels, and possibly abundant in material also. I say broadcasting, but I include the various forms of so-called narrowcasting which appear before the viewer on the same screen, though they emerge from a variety of companies and technologies. There exists a case for a national programme-making centre using television channels so long as these remain dominant modes of communication, and that must mean for many decades yet. Once programmes are made and used, however, they have today a variety of possible after-uses through the new technologies. Now, one further great virtue of the licence fee is that it is available directly to make programmes; the great vice of what I call the transactional systems of electronic communication is that the payment made by the viewer is used first to cover the cost of exhibition and distribution. In the case of cinema, the first person to be paid is the cinema proprietor, the second is the distributor, while the producer stands at the back of the queue and hopes to make a profit, if at all, only from a large range of products taken together. The producer stands in the same place in the queue in satellite, cable and video, where distribution takes up a very large proportion of the customer's payment.

The licence fee has been a wonderful programme-making revenue because the other elements of the system do not take priority. But the licence fee would be undermined in this respect if it were to be frittered away on the hardware and the technology of expensive distribution systems. The concentration of the licence fee within the BBC conceived primarily as a national programme-making centre, with other companies and other channels competing around it, is among the greatest of arguments for our existing system. The real issues of today are the nature of the future BBC, within the proliferating world of new technologies, the priorities which its management enunciates, the purposes which it announces to the world. A vast reinterpretation of the BBC is necessary – a re-dedication is how I would put it – not a dismantling.

What *should* be a matter of public discussion is the stewardship of the BBC, the choices which it has made over the last decades, and its planning for the future. We should not be engaged, as we are, in the shadow of the Peacock Committee, in an argument over whether to add advertising revenue to a rather high licence fee. Broadcasting has evolved a variety of modes of operation, the BBC's vast mega-production house being but one of them – and in the next stage of my argument I should like to look back at the evolution of some of these.

If you look through the history of radio and television in this country, you can detect two great watersheds, separating three great eras. I like to call them the three cultural systems of broadcasting, though these are not to be confused with the three ages of broadcasting of which Brian Wenham eloquently speaks in his recent book. The first era was one of the total institution, during which Reith sought to construct a BBC which itself recruited, trained and employed all those who provided the material of the broadcasts. The BBC constructed eleven house orchestras. It had its own repertory company of actors. It employed many of the major writers of the time on its staff. When confronted with problems of religious doctrine, it published its own hymn book. When looking at the problem of dialect, it established its own idiom of pure English. In the field of engineering it tried for a long time to create or modify all its own technology. It even attempted to develop video-recording, on its own, in its workshops. There are vestiges of this now curious approach at work even in the present day.

This approach, however, collapsed under the impact of the new cultural pluralism of the 1960s. It was simply impossible for the BBC to sustain a totalistic attitude towards every strand of the culture in this no longer homogeneous society. It had to admit pop music and rock to its schedules. Where Reith might have tried to hire staff rock groups, the BBC of the Greene era established the compromise of Radio 1. Where Reith tried to fit the range of national tastes into an evaluative pyramid of services – Home, Light and Third – the Greene era developed a policy of cultural outreach; it invaded the cultural ghettoes in the search for talent. It harnessed a wider range of energies, but enveloped them in the BBC. The irreverence of the mid-sixties was incorporated into the then daring late-night programme, *That Was the Week That Was*. The toddlers' truce, that period in the early evening when television disappeared from the screen, to help parents put their children to bed, was filled with magazine programmes which attempted to colonise the multitudinous trends of audience taste through a pot-pourri of snippets. But above all, the Greene era, the second cultural system, as I call it, recognised that the harnessing of an intelligentsia could not be undertaken in the Reith mode, though its harnessing was still essential for the political protection of the BBC and the development of the medium itself. The BBC, and the ITV companies also, perhaps indeed led by them, deliberately sought out the new talent. The ITV companies fostered a different style among their producers. Rather than searching for writers who would work within the system of prescribed values, the new BBC of the 1960s, competing with the first commercial channel, reversed the doctrine and sought out the writers, in the knowledge that they would shape a new set of cultural values for the institution. Johnny Speight could not be truly co-opted. Nor could Potter. Nor could David Mercer. The BBC started to work within the community of writers as a great impresario, and with remarkable results. The Wednesday play was the Globe Theatre of the period. The BBC assimilated the implications of the new cultural system, and after publication of the document *Broadcasting in the Seventies*, started to dismantle some of the more unworkable parts of its heritage.

The third of my systems of patronage is the one inaugurated by the Annan Committee and Channel 4, a system based upon the recognition that society is a kind of cauldron of activities, controversies, aspirations, talents, and that it is the task of broadcasting to turn the vexations into opportunities, to go out and seek, not talent so much as meaning and message, not to recruit already existing ability to make programmes, so much as register situations which should be transmuted into programme material, in fact evolve talent in a different way. The rubric innovation, which is crucial to the personality of Channel 4, is a term capable of expressing both much and little; Channel 4 has used it to develop new strands of expression, has sought out the unexpressed, has stimulated not just half-suppressed communities, but has given them the confidence to use the medium of television as if it were theirs. It is a task which Channel 4 has initiated, but which is capable of still wider exploration. Indeed, I think that the commissioning of independents represents a third cultural system, because I think the process can and will transform the entire face of broadcasting, not as an additional option, but as a new dynamic force. It seems to me that the public service broadcasting of the future will build upon the relatively small and new independent movement of today. It is sometimes treated, correctly, as one part of a television industry. It is already more than that. It is on the way to being a new institution of the society. A relationship between licence fee and independent community is the necessary next stop in the transformation of television itself. It will take many years only because the BBC will take many years to convert and will have to transform its whole system and arrangement of staff and resources to adapt. The proposal is not one of convenience, it is not meant to be. What is at root being proposed is a different kind of television, the introduction of a range of new professionalism, if you like – a different management imbued with different motivations. The BBC of the future would not, however, be an unhistoric transformation of the present body, but a continuation.

When you take, for example, the Corporation's galvanising role in spreading the use of the computer through this country, you see how a national institution, using television, can play a strategic role in a society. There are many such examples – perhaps the current Doomsday Project is among them – where the BBC, by reason of its whole history and position, is able to undertake major interventions in the life of a society, way beyond the mere provision of a series of programmes.

I am not just saying that the BBC should or could solve all its problems by commissioning works from small groups and independent companies. I am suggesting a considerable reorientation of the BBC, a shifting in its whole stance towards audience and society, a switch from an organisation whose chief end-product sometimes seems to be its own continuation to one which sees its role as that of making a series of interventions, using radio and television, in the life of a society.

Perhaps there is no area in which the institutional self-orientedness of the BBC is more aptly illustrated than in the matter of television archiving. It is an area in which I must, as the person responsible for the national collection of moving images in my day-to-day capacity, declare an interest and you may wish either to discount or perhaps give greater credence to what I have to say on that account. The BBC, as the major national television institution, has accumulated over fifty years the largest historical repository of moving image documents in this or any other society. On several occasions official committees and influential individuals have pleaded with the Corporation to acknowledge that its collection is more than the private production library of a television company. After a period of time historical records of any kind become progressively social, national or even international property. In the moment of its origination the Magna Carta was a local legal document – it has now become a major relic of international historical significance. Such is the way of all signifying artefacts which encompass representations of life and manners. These collections of artefacts continue to surrender their encoded store of meaning over the centuries. We use them and we honour them in the process of registering ourselves as members of a continuing civilisation.

The Corporation has argued that its sole responsibility towards its collection was that of an organisation which might need to use the material in future programmes. Access has been denied. Attempts by other friendly parties to create an access service on behalf of the BBC have been solemnly rejected. The BBC's argument in its own defence is extremely important to my general argument in this lecture, for its says that the licence is provided for the purpose of making programmes and cannot be used for the purpose of creating what would become an accessible national resource, available presumably far beyond the BBC itself. Recently Stephen Hearst, an advisor to the Director-General on policy matters, has argued in the *Listener* that there should be a national collection of television materials accessible to television professionals so that each generation of producers should be aware of their own professional heritage. Of course he is right. It would be an important advance. But why is this massive heritage the moral property of one profession of a few hundred people? Why should it not be acknowledged as a major source of national and international history? Of course, the rules of copyright would not permit access to be developed as easily as to the national collections of books or music. But the performing unions have long now recognised archival and cultural rights to the after use of their members' work. There exists with the National Film (and Television) Archive a growing, though terribly inadequate, collection of television programmes and the uses to which this is being put, even within the proper but painful constraints of copyright, are both inspiring and instructive. Progress will continue to occur. The ITV companies and Channel 4 have been slowly building up with the National Film (and Television) Archive a wonderful collection of their work.

On 1 January 1985 NFA established a new basis for the collection and one can now say in respect of those two channels that for the last six months little, if anything, which should have been kept has been lost. All of it is being preserved at broadcast standard, as well as on inexpensive and easily available cassettes. Does the BBC really have to refuse to participate? And because of the licence fee? The licence fee is not a payment for a production company, but surely the foundation stone of a national resource; the licence fee rather than a justification for not archiving offers, it seems to me, a reverse argument – it provides by its nature an obligation on the receiving organisation to operate precisely as a national resource. The BBC's treatment of archiving as an excrescence or luxurious irrelevance illustrates the way in which it is habitually unable to recognise its own historical achievement. In insisting that it is really just one part of an industry and that it must always appear to be prudently cheese-paring it is selling itself short.

The licence fee places the BBC irrevocably inside the public sector, but insulated from government. What we pay for through our licence is the BBC's liberty, because that under-pins our own liberty. The greatest thing the BBC offers us is *its* independence. We need it to be strong in the sense of being invulnerable to political and commercial interference; we do not want it to behave as a private bastion. Its haughti-ness, which has increased exasperatingly with the years, is a denial of the true purposes of its independence. The BBC, as the principal instrument of public service broadcasting, requires its strength to withstand attack, not to protect an interest. Politicians should feel free to attack it but know that it will reach its own judgements on policy. Its largeness and wealth are necessary so that it will never cynically incline to the wishes of the powerful. It has seldom done so. But its financial weakness in the present decade, allied to its incessant desire to enter and dominate every field, makes it more and more likely that one day it will fall victim to the depredations of an unscrupulous politician. The more often the BBC is obliged to press the Prime Minister of the day for rises in the licence fee, the more politically vulnerable it renders itself.

There are various ways in which one can order the elements of the argument about the BBC's independence. Licence fee, political pressure, inflation, growth of services, size of staff, public service – those are the elements. Does the BBC need to undertake every branch of broadcasting and narrowcasting in order to maintain the size of its audience overall, in order to have the licence fee raised, in order to pursue independent courses of action? I believe the argument works the other way round. The BBC offers us its independence of operation as the chief return on our annual investment in the licence fee; the larger the increase it demands, the more politically vulnerable it renders itself. It follows, therefore, that it should operate always within a licence fee that is not excessively politically contentious. The BBC's scope should be defined by the available fee, not the other way round. It should not expand its staff beyond the number necessary to operate as the supreme national institution of broadcasting. As the new media arrive, it should, more and more, stick to its task of programme-making and not seek to operate one transmission technology after another. Its programmes could well, in any case, take up a major part of the channels of cable and satellite, and not only in Britain. The BBC's chief resource is its staff and the way in which its extraordinary range of responsibilities increase their skills. But it must recognise also the way in which the skills and professions which make the moving image are now spreading across the country and are no longer held within one or two institutions. The power of the licence fee is just as great if exercised via outside commissions as via in-house production. The freedoms which are conferred by the licence fee are capable of being spread and multiplied. The authority of the BBC is not attenuated through the provision of work to independent companies. On the contrary, the BBC, if it operated indeed as a great national foundation, would be helping to sustain the levels of excellence, the spread of voices, the cultural nourishment of the nation. Wherever television programmes are being made, there should the BBC be, offering resources, protection, experience, influence. Wherever national policy is being discussed, in the ethnic communities, in the new cinema industry, in the cable industry, in the satellite industry, there the BBC should be, looking for opportunities to help, to make strategic interventions, to experiment, to collaborate, never simply to incorporate nor to dominate. I am trying to suggest an alternative line of corporate development, not put a plan to cut back, to economise, to make do. I am suggesting a reinterpretation of the BBC's political, moral and cultural purposes to suit a period of time – our time – in which the use of moving images is no longer the mysterious exclusive property of one agency or two, but a general means of communication. I am suggesting a vast range of new roles and new skills, new places in which the BBC should appear as stimulator, animator. I am suggesting that it abandon the policies of the fortress, and I am suggesting that the licence

fee, in its purest form, unadulterated with advertising, is the
most important democratic instrument we possess.

In fact, the BBC and television generally have probably
been the greatest of the instruments of social democracy of
the century, more important than the health service, than
national insurance, than the state education system com-
bined. We spend more time with television than we do, as
children, with our teachers. We spend more years watching
television than we do drawing our pensions. The medium
dominates the sources of the message and its penumbral
power is vast and barely understood. Somewhere in the space
between the audience and the screen, representations turn
into realities. To describe and analyse these processes will be
the work of many researchers, most of them not yet born.

Amid the swirling changes in technology and in prevailing
doctrines, we have to hold fast to the rock of public service
broadcasting. We need the established institutions because
they either are or can be rendered accountable. Through
them we, the inhabitants of the society, will have some access
to the new and still little understood processes by which
societies are today controlled. That is why we need the BBC
more than ever before to carry out its fundamental mission
still. But to do so it will have to undertake massive and continuous self-reform. The other institutions of broadcasting
and the new devices will indeed only find their true role in
the new conditions when the BBC has found its.

The BBC and the concept of public service broadcasting

Like Brenda Maddox, it is probably best for me to write about what I know about from my own perspective, that of somebody who has worked in Whitehall with politicians and officials and as a member of the public who is interested in the notion of political culture and in what it means to be a member of a society. That may be one way of helping to answer the question which David Elstein has asked apropos the former Home Secretary's remarks about broadcasting. David asked Lord Whitelaw, 'What's it got to do with you?' Of course, the shape and financing of broadcasting in this country has certainly 'got to do' with politicians, whether we like it or not.

Now, what I do at the BBC is to ask a question which I ask people at each organisation for which I work: 'What's going on here?' This is generally an unwelcome question but I believe it to be a useful and necessary one. What I see at the BBC and what a great many outsiders, including politicians and officials, see is something identified years ago by the scientist Sir Edward Appleton. 'An organisation', he said, 'takes five years to grow, five years to do its best work, and five years to die.' Perhaps one could lengthen this: say, twenty years to grow, twenty years to do its best work, twenty years to die, and although even that may seem cruel, the general principle is obvious. Organisations do have lives. They do go through phases and the BBC is no exception. It is suffering from the sclerosis that tends eventually to affect all institutions and organisations. After some sixty years this is not surprising. In his address Anthony Smith spoke of Max Weber, who gave one of the first descriptions of 'bureaucracy'. The BBC is a very good example of a bureaucratic organisation. Its affairs are run in carefully delegated ways, each level of the hierarchy, from the top of the pyramid to the wide layers at the bottom, having its own degree of discretion in decision-making. There is a very definite hierarchy and, the further up you go, the more mystique each superior level enjoys. The BBC shares the defensiveness of all bureaucratic organisations, with the appropriate secretiveness, too. That secretiveness and mystery is protected and enhanced by the use of jargon, in particular the use of initials, to baffle the outsider. There is much emphasis on team spirit and the whole operation is infused with an interesting mixture of arrogance and panic, plus a degree of paranoia. As in all sixty-year-old bureaucracies, too, the inhabitants have a slight suspicion that they have become boring and that their arguments are boring.

May I offer you a parallel? It is the nuclear industry which, though this may strike you as odd, has quite a lot in common with the broadcasting industry. It is about the same age, it was for a long time an expanding industry, and was more or less left to get on with the duties that were delegated to it by politicians and officers. Like broadcasting, the nuclear industry enjoyed a degree of glamour, because what it did was mysterious and rather strange to laymen. Furthermore, just as broadcasters have cherished their editorial independence, so in the nuclear industry enormous importance has been attached to intellectual independence. These two industries have now reached that point in the life of an organisation – it happens to people too, and to governments and prime ministers – where they become accident-prone, where the mystique and glamour begin to wear thin. You may wonder why I am talking about the BBC as if it is a living thing, as if it is an organism, rather than an organisation. We all do so. (Indeed, I have noticed that Anthony Smith speaks of the BBC as 'it'; David Elstein, perhaps understandably, as 'them'.) The BBC, like other organisations, encourages this attitude. But living things die – in this country we have seen a great many apparently immortal institutions die, great industries like the railways and the steamships, for example. In the commercial world it is easier to tell when something is, if not dead, moribund, because the state of the balance sheet shows when life is draining away. With an organisation like the BBC, however, you can never be quite sure when brain death has actually occurred. There we have no balance sheet, no simple criteria of success or failure. Producers and managers, like all human beings, search endlessly for ways of measuring how well they are doing. The ratings are little use; the test is much more in whether or not there is a general feeling of success, of esteem. The BBC is not the only organisation whose members depend on such woolly tests. The National Health Service, the universities – all such organisations have similar problems with trying to measure how well they are doing. In any case, for all the government's efforts to draw up criteria based on social transfers and such like, how do we know what is meant by 'doing well'? The assessment of success is to a large extent not measureable. That is the reason why it is hard to tell how lively – or not – the BBC actually remains.

There is a second reason, which has very much to do with the BBC's method of funding. In his chapter Anthony Smith describes the BBC licence fee as a poll-tax but in fact nobody is really sure what sort of a charge the licence fee represents. Even the Treasury is divided into those who say it is a poll-tax and those who say it is some sort of subscription. Perhaps we can most usefully think of it as a special sort of tax, unusual for this country in that it is a hypothecated tax, attached in this case to a bit of hardware. It is rather like the road fund licence was meant to be, a tax whose proceeds are devoted, after some deduction for the cost of collection and for duty, to the carrying on of the service in question, rather than being put into the Consolidated Fund and then dispensed among government departments and agencies in proportions decided upon by civil servants and ministers. This is really the core of the BBC's present difficulties. An organisation which relies on a hypothecated tax of this sort must justify its legitimacy, and for this its managers must take care to satisfy several sets of people. (All these add up to what has been described today as the society or the political culture or whatever, but I will come back to that in a minute.) Who are these sets? One lot is composed of people of the official sort; the second lot is the public and the third lot are ministers.

Let us start with officials. Officials hate hypothecated taxes, which 'confuse the picture'. Such taxes to an important extent diminish civil servants' discretion as to how money collected from the public should be allocated. This is why, whenever the Treasury has the opportunity, its officials mouth what they believe to be (and in some cases are) ministers' beliefs: that 'it is not fair for consumers who should have a right to spend their money as they wish'. And officials continue: 'It is not fair that consumers should be obliged to pay this tax just because they have a television; nor is it fair that the money should automatically go to the BBC.'

What about the public and the politicians? It is also important for the BBC to satisfy the public as to the legitimacy of this particular tax, because that is what you have to do with taxes. As for the politicians, the BBC has to satisfy them because otherwise they will make the loudest fuss, either in order to stand well with their civil servants or to stand well with the public, or both, depending on how they sniff the wind at any particular time.

Now in different ways the BBC has gone about reassuring people that it should be funded in this special way. How has it done so? I remember being told about this when I first went to advise the BBC. As Anthony Smith himself told me: 'There is one thing you must understand about the BBC: they make mistakes over and over again but they have enormous guile. At the last moment, whatever the crisis, they always produce a decision or an announcement or a manoeuvre and they invariably actually survive.' Anthony is right. It has been by means of such guile, which many of us admire but simultaneously find rather off-putting, that the BBC has actually managed to retain the approval of these groups of people – the officials, the public and the politicians – and has sustained the legitimacy of the licence fee device.

It has done so in three ways, which I shall call the decent way, the heroic, and the quasi-scientific way. First the decent way. As I noticed when I first went to be looked over by the BBC, the organisation is full of extremely decent men and women, not, except mildly here and there, at all megalomaniacal but good, sound, solid, thoughtful citizens. Moreover, these men and women and their organisation have also, perhaps intuitively, drawn upon and copied what is considered decent and reasonable behaviour by those whose good will they need. Thus the BBC admittedly squares itself with officials by, for instance, adopting after some lapse of time, whatever techniques of management have recently been fashionable in Whitehall – one moment delegated authority, the next financial management initiatives (called by the BBC 'activity reviews'). Another example. When it suits the BBC, the organisation adopts what it considers to be the style of Whitehall. Take archives policy, which Anthony has near to his heart. Until recently the BBC's archive policy, was, as Stephen Hearst described it, more or less one of search and destroy. Every now and then a list of programmes would be circulated to heads of department who would mark those that might be deleted – in Stephen's case, his own programmes especially, since he was anxious to 'set a good example'. This was very like Whitehall practice, as I remember from my time in the think-tank, whose archive was saved more by good luck than by design. Today, just as Whitehall is beginning to recognise the importance of its archive (rechristened data base) for the operation and memory of the organisation, so – or at least we hope so – is the BBC. By changing its spots, chameleon-like, BBC bureaucrats accommodate themselves to the appearance and habits of the bureaucrats whose backing they need.

A slightly different tactic is used to retain the goodwill of the public, to legitimise there the existence and working of the licence fee. Here the BBC has survived by providing something for everyone in its programming, by appealing to each majority and minority group and to every combination of them all. Just as a speaker who wants to keep the attention of his audience will have a remark for each sector or opinion, will quote each view, so the BBC balances the requirements of each constituent part of its whole audience. There is a bit of intellectualism, a bit of pseudo-intellectualism, and, as I discovered when I arrived, a good deal of anti-intellectualism. There is extreme vulgarity (look at the *Radio Times*) and there is a more lofty side. At best this is reassuring, at worst it is confusing. It can easily seem to be manipulation to the utmost degree, which of course it is.

And the politicians? By and large they are reassured by the BBC's reminding them, when it can, that it is not financed by 'public money' but by the public's money and that anyway the BBC is a national institution which is doing everything a national institution is expected to do. That, incidentally, is partly why the BBC has found itself embarking on some of the ventures for which it has been most criticised, local radio being one, the DBS project another. I think you will see what I am driving at. The BBC has until now managed to square these different constituencies by being pretty sensitive to the prevailing wind outside the organisation. It has been sensitive, too, to its own workings, constantly reviewing its own procedures and conventions. All this is to some extent a gamble. It requires the BBC to judge and to steer a

delicate course between what it thinks people expect and
what it thinks they want. This is now an almost impossible
task. It is now very hard to satisfy officials. In Whitehall there
is a mania for precision but the BBC's legitimacy depends
on a necessary imprecision – it has to persuade each group
that it *in particular* is being addressed most of the time, something even the most subtle audience measurement techniques
cannot do. The Civil Service is itself demoralised and therefore less keen on sticking up for an organisation that, understandably, sometimes seems to be demoralised too. What is
more, both the popular consensus and the political consensus
that have sustained the BBC's method of financing seem,
perhaps only temporarily, to have gone. Unlike Japan, of
which Brenda Maddox writes, in Britain the public and
politicians do not share a common view of what constitutes
our society's principles and beliefs. We are more conscious
of what separates the groups in our society than of what
unites us. That, as much as anything, makes 'the decent way',
or as the Japanese might put it, 'the honourable way', an
inadequate basis on which to sustain what strives to be a
national institution.

And so we fall back upon the heroic way, rather like the
Latin-American General who constantly stood for election
in whichever Latin-American country it was, with only the
one slogan, the one plank in his political platform: 'Give me
a balcony and I will be President.' In such a fashion has the
BBC from time to time relied upon charismatic managers or
charismatic governors, who for a while have allowed it to
carry people along, carry the public along, on a great adventure on which all might be convinced that they were engaged.
John Reith managed to do it, Hugh Greene, Huw Wheldon
managed to do it; Jeremy Isaacs has done it at Channel 4.
There are, however, few men and women of this sort available
in an organisation at any particualr time. It is difficult for
people of this sort to survive in organisations, for they are
disinclined to struggle up the ranks of a hierarchy. They

would rather leave and do something else. Moreover, it is a considerable strain to be led by such people for more than a short time. They are demanding, they drive everyone before them. The only way in which such pressure can be borne is by alternating the heroes and heroines with ordinary, unassuming leaders.

If the decent way depends on a consensus that is lacking, and if we are in uncharismatic times, what course remains by which the BBC may retain support for itself? There is only the quasi-scientific way. By 'scientifically' measuring, say, audience ratings, value for money, (whatever that may mean), allocation of resources, feedback, and all the rest of it, can the BBC prove to its three constituencies – officials, politicians and the public – that it is doing what it should?

The problem is that none of these measures is satisfactory or convincing and anyway – and I shall finish here – you cannot measure the most vital thing – you cannot measure legitimacy. The question to which there is no enduring answer, only a series of guesses, is whether this society is one in which, as a people, we believe that, in addition to other methods of producing and disseminating information, education and entertainment, we want and believe we ought to have a BBC, an ITV and a Channel 4. David Elstein has reminded us that this is a question about judgements: what 'ought' we to have? Who 'ought' to decide what we, as a people, 'ought' to have?

Some aspects of our society depend chiefly upon a notion of altruism. The point of the licence fee system of financing the BBC is *exactly* that one pays the fee whether or not one watches BBC programmes. Just, in fact, as people give blood or pay their NHS contributions, whether or not they use the health service. It is harder to make the case – though I believe it is time to do so – for a society's needing the sort of broadcasting system we have, by miraculous chance, developed in this country than it is to further the case of having a national health service. It is because of the difficulty of making that case, particularly to determined sceptics, that the BBC has been exploring other methods by which broadcasting might be financed. Unlike some engineers, especially some BBC engineers, there are those who envisage a system by which television signals might be scrambled, with viewers buying a decoding device (an 'intelligent credit card', for instance) by which they might unscramble the channel signal. Such a system of subscribing to receive a channel would answer the objections of those who believe that 'compulsion' nullifies altruism. Such a system might be practicable within five to ten years – but the problems have little to do with practicality. The fundamental issue is, rather, one about universality, for the underlying principles on which the broadcasting system has been based in this country have been, hitherto, those of universality – wherever a viewer or a listener lives, he or she has been able to receive the signal, at the same price as is paid by any other person, and it has been a signal carrying *all* offerings, from which anyone may choose. The test now is to reconcile those principles of universality with the selectivity which subscription brings.

What do we do in the meantime? I will simply make three points. First, the BBC must be much more sensitive to the society from which it seeks its cash. It needs to question its own assumptions much more readily, to be more porous. The mechanisms for sensing what the public wants and how the public feels are beginning to creak and they need early lubrication. One means might be by requiring all BBC employees to leave after ten years and not to return, if at all, for two. My second thought concerns the notion of choice. Broadcasters might usefully remind those – politicians especially – who talk of 'more choice' that a proliferation of channels does not necessarily widen choice. 'Choice among what?' one may well ask, for choices have ultimately to be made. All the technology and time shifting in the world will not bring more that twenty-four hours in the day; incomes will for most people never be limitless. People will always have to choose among what is offered; it is more useful to ensure, as well as we can, that they are able to choose among several good things than among a vast quantity of trash. And, last, I would suggest that we need a little more plain speaking. In Japan the broadcasters and the public enjoy a contractual relationship; here the broadcasters are entitled to do their stuff by the terms of a Charter and Licence, in the case of the BBC, and an Act of Parliament in the IBA's case. [The Charter and Licence have served the BBC well in the past, the relationship between the Corporation and the government has been loose and, while the parties wanted it so, vague. It has resembled a marriage between two people who are from time to time unfaithful, but who have found it easier to carry on and live with the existing arrangements because any alternative would be worse.] Disruption is anyway difficult and awkward; it consumes time and energy. but there sometimes comes a moment when such a relationship seems false, or strikes observers as dishonest and mutually exploitative. Is this actually the way both parties wish to live? Perhaps it is, but they must say so openly. This is the moment when the marriage counsellor walks in observing that all is not well. That role is now being played by Professor Peacock and his committee. This, then, is the time when we must all say what we think the relationship has been and should be – all of us, BBC people, non-BBC people, and the politicians. It is not enough for the politicians to put upon the broadcasters the burden of justifying existing arrangements; they too must put the case, whether for continuity or change. The issue is not one of technology or economics but of politics, of how as a society we wish to use our joint resources and collectively manage our affairs.

Centralisation and censorship

What follows is a collection of comments on key areas of conflict in culture and communication, and questions of change and control arising from a lecture by Anthony Smith on the BBC and public service broadcasting, which opened the John Logie Baird seminar (Chapter 1 in this book).

This contribution to the debate comes from a consumer, from a listener and a viewer, with no inside knowledge of television production but with a keen interest in what is produced and, equally, what is not produced. Like all interventions mine is a political one and partial in both senses of the word – piecemeal and partisan. The starting point for this intervention will be that the BBC has, since its very inception, operated as a powerful political force in our society and that consequently all efforts to promote it as an apolitical institution are based on false premises.

It is not simply a question of the BBC bowing to political pressure: the BBC is itself a product and a producer of political pressure. It is both subject to and capable of exerting political pressure. The primary fault of the spirited defences of the BBC, conducted by confirmed believers in public service broadcasting, is that they fail to acknowledge that it was from the very beginning bound up with a programme of prejudice, both political and national. It was not merely susceptible to sporadic interference from specific political factions but was precisely a profoundly political organisation marked as much by its outcasts as its broadcasts. Thus I am not simply concerned with what the BBC does, with what it puts out on the air and on the screen, but also with what it refuses to reveal, such as the dubiety of its own origins.

Reith was, of course, quite correct when he likened the BBC to a national church; it is an ideological state apparatus which most certainly serves its function of creating the illusion of social cohesion and political integration in the midst of difference and disintegration. The BBC is both powerful and political and it is very often the powerless who bow to its wishes. We only have to think of the reporting of Ireland, the Falklands War or the miners' strike to comprehend that the BBC operates not merely as a transmitter of messages, as a disseminator of a neutral web of news and information, but as a producer of highly selective text and images designed to present a specific view of 'British' society and the struggles waged within it. The unwaged are not party to the politics of the nation; there is no national interest in their account or in their condition, only in their conditioning and in the 'British broadcasting culture' which swamps them. Who controls the medium, controls the production and distribution of 'truth' and 'meaning'.

Anthony Smith's own public broadcast was effectively a rearguard action in defence of the BBC in the face of increasingly overt political pressure from the right. He was quite determined not to express the extent to which the BBC has always been prey to covert political pressure. Government propaganda is not simply required in time of crises such as the Korean conflict, Suez or Bloody Sunday, it must be produced in the most subtle and pervasive manner throughout the year. The braying of liberal humanism reaches a crescendo only when the national chauvinism and political bias of the BBC are stepped up in moments of political instability. If we were given free and unrestricted access to BBC archives we might uncover some excruciatingly partisan material. This is perhaps why the archives are so difficult to penetrate. Television, like the national press, deals in the sort of daily truths

which prove embarrassing to their purveyors when subsequent events invalidate them.

Those who allege that criticism of the special instances of
BBC bias ignores the fact that its principal role is as a mass
entertainer stretch our imagination to its very limits.
Anthony Smith's failure to link the images and text of current
affairs programmes to the images and text of entertainment
is reprehensible. Drama and entertainment play as much a
part in 'educating' the populace as news and current affairs.
He then attempts to apologise for those 'special' instances
by contending that the BBC had as its points of comparison
the radio networks of Hitler and Mussolini. We do not have
to go that far back to trace BBC bias. Kissinger recently
stated that had he possessed the servile media which Mrs
Thatcher had at her disposal during the Falklands Crisis, he
might not have encountered such opposition to his policies
in south-east Asia. Anthony Smith has no right to criticise
the American system when our own national press and television networks print or screen almost nothing detrimental
to the well-being of the present political order.

On another plane we should consider the BBC not merely
as a centralising producer of culture and disseminator of
information but also as a censoring body, as a system of
channels and levers which control, organise and exclude the
passage of text and image in our society. It is thanks to the
BBC that the line between terrorism and democracy is so
clearly drawn. Transparency and clarity are primary concerns
of the British broadcasting system. Directness and opacity
are its priorities. None of this materiality of language or
power of discourse nonsense. The BBC deals in plain truths.
A close-up of Stephen McConomy's head on the *Nine O'Clock
News* and a rundown of the effects of the impact of an anti-
personnel plastic cartridge on the skull of a child are outside
the normal audio-visual economy of the BBC. A close-up of
the contorted face of the Secretary of State for Trade and
Industry on his exit from the Grand Hotel in Brighton is

good television and much more in line with government thinking.

The political factor, however, is not the only one which promoters of public service broadcasting minimise or misinterpret. There is also the national factor. The BBC is above all a 'British' institution, and this national identity has a politically tendentious dimension in Belfast and Brixton, both 'British', but not as 'British' as the BBC. When people such as Melvyn Bragg or Anthony Smith present the BBC as a great national institution being subjected to unwelcome political pressures from outside, they paint too simplistic a picture. The political and national dimensions which play upon public service broadcasting are not outside it anymore than they are outside the nation, although the fear of an American invasion via satellite bombardment brings out British national chauvinism and permits professors of the merits of the British system to portray the real threat as 'out there'. An interesting instance of this paranoia occurs in a text entitled *Television: Technology and Cultural Form* by Raymond Williams. The author delivers the apocalyptic warning that satellite television might precipitate external control of domestic broadcasting by powerful paranational companies. Presumably paranational companies are a more dangerous parasite than national ones, especially when their host is the great national church which the BBC constitutes.

The well-being of the BBC has always been dependent upon the turn of events outside the 'nation' it purports to serve. I am not at the moment in possession of the full facts and figures for the BBC with regard to its genesis, but I would hazard a guess that the possibility of its expansion and development, indeed, the very condition for its existence, coincided with the need for a new definition of the nation: a politico-cultural centre which could hold the lines of force which deviate therefrom. The BBC was the revelation of Reith which would reinforce the national grid. In the wake of the scramble for colonies, the first imperialist war, the growth of American capital and the partition of Ireland, it was evident that 'Britishness' was not simply something present and permanent, it was something to be produced in a continual process of cultural reformation. The BBC does not reflect or represent an already fully-formed national consciousness, a coherent national identity, rather it is one of several material agents or 'national' institutions which produce and reproduce that very identity. The BBC is both national and political, and it is the politics of its nationality and the nationality of its politics which must be questioned.

In his defence of the BBC, Anthony Smith says: 'All one can say to define the indefinable nature of the BBC is that it is a national institution.' Anyone, however, who disagrees with the precise boundaries of the nation within which that institution is located will be designated an extremist or a terrorist in its news coverage. All one can say to define the indefinable nature of the BBC is that words like 'nation' and 'nature' took on a special significance some time in the sixteenth century as adumbrated by Raymond Williams in his *Keywords*. The key to the BBC lies in its role as the voice or vision of the British nation. As a national institution it institutes an audio-visual impression of national unity wholly at odds with political, historical, economic and social realities. It provides the London government with the possibility of a unified utterance which denies the diffracted constituency of its vast fiefdom. The BBC operates in conjunction with the state education system as the ideological state apparatus responsible for delineating the lines of development of standard English. Linguistic lines of force pulsate outwards from London via education, television, radio and newspapers. While the hegemony of the BBC persists there will be a proper way to speak, a language of transparency and clarity, the voice of pure reason. BBC English is exactly the speech of vision.

But to what extent is the BBC a national institution? A precise formulation of this question would at once destroy nine-tenths of Anthony Smith's arguments. The BBC is a national institution in so far as it consistently promotes the illusion of a unified and integrated political region with a system of common values and beliefs. It is very existence perpetuates this myth.

The term 'unity' is frequently employed in defence of the BBC. Anthony Smith returns again and again to the question of the BBC's place in society as a powerful and independent unitary institution; although he believes that the BBC has compromised on its special ideals forged in its founding era and has contracted some sort of amnesia regarding its role as a national resource. We must not forget, however, that it is the monolithic unity constituted by the BBC which enables an integrated vision of our society to cover every region in the country. Unlike the USA, where local and regional television networks predominate and where the cinema is the truly national medium, Britain relies heavily upon the BBC as a specifically national media institution to strengthen the myth of a unified nation. The BBC is ethnocentric, phallocentric, logocentric and just plain centric.

Anthony Smith is generous in his praise of one particular alternative to the BBC. '. . . Channel 4 has sought out the unexpressed, has stimulated not just half-suppressed communities but has given them the confidence to use the medium of television as if it were theirs.' What are these half-suppressed communities doing in our free, unified society? Should the medium of television belong to those who control it or to those who provide the wealth which permits its existence in the first place? Confidence comes with real participation, not subsequent to some series of half-hearted reforms. Perhaps the Irish community would wish to express its objections to the notion of a single nation covered by a single broadcasting outlet. Only the complete and utter dissolution of the monolithic structure which is the BBC will permit the proliferation of local centres of communication and cultural development. A reformation of that great national church will simply prolong the agony and allow 'the powers that be' to regroup behind a slimmer, fitter BBC which professes to being prepared to tolerate and indeed encourage a relaxation of its monopoly. Such cosmetic revision must not blur the focus of those determined to witness the installation of a truly democratic communications framework in our society. The kind of overhaul proposed by Anthony Smith is aimed at pre-empting criticism of the BBC which demands that it be dismantled and scrapped in favour of local cultural communes or, to be more precise, in favour of a system of communications which radically challenged the cultural centrality of London and the south-east of England and triggered off a political disintegration which threatened the national unity which was the 'founding stone' of the BBC.

But let us proceed to the nature of the whole heterogeneous business. The BBC is a business, similar to religion or education. Its profits are political capital. It deals in discourse, culture and communication. By reproducing and developing, even by reforming, the dominant ideology, the BBC produces profits in terms of the perpetuation of the political system which permits, tolerates and limits its existence. One has only to give a little thought to the governmental and also the general economic, social and every other kind of dependence of modern, educated people on the ruling bourgeoisie to realise that any and all talk of the BBC's independence constitutes an obstacle in the path of a radical demythification of the media.

Anthony Smith has the audacity to commence his discussion of the licensing mechanism by asserting that '. . .It is temporarily fashionable in Britain to analyse everything in terms of money, as if income and expenditure represented the reality of things rather than a measure of them'. If Anthony had read his namesake Adam, he may have discovered that it has been fashionable to analyse everything in terms of money since the transformation of this country into a society based upon the power of capital, a society in which the possession of money constitutes the only real liberty. Discourse is a marketable commodity, of course, as well as being a source of power and a means of attaining it; and Anthony Smith's discourse is powerful in that it is not simply a diagnosis of the state of the media but a programme for reforming the media of the State. Here I could mention Grindal and the transference of power from the pulpit to the lectern in relation to the analogy of the Church and the BBC. I could speak of Cambridge, indeed of Oxbridge, with reference to the gestation of a new professional priesthood. Instead I want to explore Anthony Smith's utterances on the financial framework of the broadcasting system in Britain: '. . .it does not fit easily into normal methods of economic analysis'. What are normal methods of economic analysis? Let me provide a brief example of current normal methods of economic analysis. In 1974 the government decided to close nine secondary schools in Strathclyde in order to save £12 million. It then decided to spend £400 million on 250 Challenger tanks for deployment in West Germany. If these vehicles are not in action within the next fifteen years they will be obsolete. These are normal methods of economic analysis.

Anthony Smith comes clean when he admits that the BBC exists first by political decision, and then by a system of revenue built around it. The BBC owes its existence to a series of political decisions taken outside its control. Raymond Williams made an interesting point when he warned of the danger of the BBC becoming a separate empire. Its existence was and is based upon the existence of the British one, or rather, what is left of it. Its national status depends upon the unity of a nation which is held together not by social cohesion or economic parity but by political control and by the persistence of a powerful nation-wide network of communication, the levers of which are ultimately operated by and for those who profit from the perpetration of

the myth of unity. Anthony Smith argues for reformation
and realignment rather than transformation and disintegration. He says: 'The licence to operate is granted ultimately
by the powers that be within a society; they decide how the
service concerned is to be paid for, and on what conditions
its managers will have to work'. The truth will out. The
powers in a society can never be, they are always becoming.
Power is volatile and unstable. The maintenance of a
monolith like the BBC carries with it the hazards of a complete collapse of the central platform for the reproduction of
the dominant ideology in a mature capitalist society. If we
really want democracy we should question the existence of
God rather than seeking to simply reform his Church.

Anthony Smith describes the licence fee as 'a very simple
device for funding a non-transactional medium'. The licence
fee is precisely a very complex mechanism for controlling a
framework of discursive practices and for organising and
directing the production and transmission of image and text
designed to duplicate and develop the divergent levels of the
dominant value system. Anthony Smith defines the licence
as a price fixed by the government for the upkeep of a total
service. Total here is the exact term. The licence fee permits
a degree of totalisation concomitant with the doctrine of
monopoly capitalism. The BBC is a total service which can
either be cleansed of its more overtly totalising tendencies
or against which we might initiate localised counter-
responses designed to challenge its central role in our society.
He goes on to say 'It is a poll-tax of a kind, and regressive
in a way, since rich and poor pay the same sum. . .'. So much
for national unity when the population of this free society
are divided into rich and poor. Speaking of the television
system in the USA Anthony Smith observes that '. . . it took
decades for television even to reach certain parts of the
country'. Here in Britain the BBC reaches the parts that other
instruments of social democracy cannot, such as the police,
the army and the legal and educational bodies. In Scotland,

for example, differences in religion, law and education are ironed out by the BBC. Where the baton cannot reach the signal can. The highland clearances might have been conducted more efficiently were the unfortunate crofters provided with a daily bombardment of information on the economic normality of the project.

Anthony Smith maintains that the licence serves to '. . .enhance the life of a free society through the use of a communications technology'. The licence fee serves to enable the members of an unfree society to fund a germinating political phalanx best described by the term 'techno-fascism'. The capital currently being invested in communications technology by the Conservative government is designed to cover crowd control and surveillance rather than to enhance the life of anyone. The licence is linked to taking liberties, not making them.

'The licence fee places the BBC irrevocably inside the public sector but insulated from government.' No institution in our society is insulated from government. 'What we pay for through our licence fee is the BBC's liberty, because that underpins our own liberty.' What we pay for through our licence is a stream of sexist and racist effluence interspersed with testimonies to the freedom of our society. 'Its largeness and wealth are necessary so that it will never cynically incline to the wishes of the powerful. It has seldom done so.' It has always done so. In actual fact the largeness and wealth of the BBC indicate precisely its willingness to incline to the wishes of the powerful. If it posed the slightest threat to the powerful it would be dismantled. It is exactly because it has served the rich and powerful that it has occupied such a central position in our society for so long. Only a professional individual completely insulated from the political realities of his own society could consider the BBC as a neutral national resource.

When he contends that the BBC can avoid being subjected to undue political pressure by modifying its demands for an increase in the licence fee, Anthony Smith unwittingly reveals the central contradiction in his argument. What independence can the BBC possibly enjoy when its freedom depends wholly and entirely upon decisions taken at government level, decisions which profoundly influence not simply its expansion and development but which actually affect the very flavour and tone of its output? Economic dependence upon central government has always precluded the possibility of genuine independence. The BBC has always been politically contentious. The idea that it will only submit itself to political pressure if it continues to price itself out of a job is either a calculated mystification or a total misinterpretation of the political processes and practices prevalent in our society. By arguing for stringency Anthony Smith is merely asking the BBC to do exactly what it will be compelled to do by the present government. The current spate of cutbacks will bite as hard in the area of communications as it will in the provision of health care and education. Anthony Smith supports the BBC's concern to extend its field of operations into virgin territory but cautions against any expansion in staff numbers. 'It should not expand its staff beyond the number necessary to operate as the supreme national institution of broadcasting.' The concept of more technology and less staff is one with which Mrs Thatcher agrees wholeheartedly.

Anthony Smith's worthy advice, 'Wherever national policy is being discussed, in the ethnic communities, in the new cinema industry, in the cable industry, in the satellite industry, there the BBC should be, looking for opportunities to help, to make strategic interventions, to experiment, to collaborate, never simply to incorporate, nor to dominate', is fraught with problems. The term national policy is anathema to the ethnic communities exactly because it implies a degree of socio-political cohesion absent from our multi-racial society. Coercion and assimilation are the twin towers from which the present government conducts its national policy. And, the recruiting policy of the BBC, and therefore its present composition, makes it impossible for it to be truly representative in certain areas of class, sex, race, etc., however good its intentions. The BBC is ethnocentric, Oxbridge-dominated and reactionary through and through.

Criticism always carries with it the obligation to put forward 'alternatives', as though the thing which is bad can be made good by being supplanted with a new version along similar lines. This whole idea rests on the concept of continuity and reformation, rather than discontinuity and transformation. This is what Anthony Smith advocates: 'A vast reinterpretation of the BBC is necessary – a re-dedication is how I would put it – not a dismantling'. Mrs Thatcher has no intention of dismantling the BBC although she may endeavour to 'streamline' it. I definitely detect a sense of sixteenth century puritanism – this notion of a reinterpretation of the Word. This idea of a re-dedication to some perfect vision reminds me of another reformation. Gilles Deleuze has admirably criticised the reforming impulse and alluded to the supreme insolence of those who seek to elicit public support for their representation of some fictional national will.

Anthony Smith claims that 'There exists a case for a national programme-making centre using television channels so long as these remain dominant modes of communication and that must mean for many decades'. There exists a case for combating the concept of national programmes as such. There exists a case for questioning the domination, through one-way channels of communication, of the majority of the populace by a powerful minority professing to be representative of the national interest. There exists a case for contamination and destabilisation as opposed to purification and paralysis, for disintegration rather than assimilation. There exists a case for questioning the motives of certain individuals who promote the merits of a national institution dependent upon a pervasive web of false information for that very status. There exists a case for altering the centralising propensity of our Western scopic drive and phonetic consciousness by countering the paralysed centrality of the BBC with multiple local counter-responses. There exists a case for displacing a stationary monolith with a *mélange* of stations.

'Amid the swirling changes in technology and in prevailing doctrines we have to hold fast to the rock of public service broadcasting.' Amid the strategic manoeuvres of the powers that be we must determine to smash the rock of public service broadcasting and splinter its monopoly of sound and vision. 'That is why we need the BBC more than ever before to carry out its fundamental mission still.' The project to reform this particular national Church is a mission impossible. 'But to do so it will have to undertake massive and continuous self-reform.' 'The other institutions of broadcasting and the new devices will indeed only find their true role in the new conditions, when the BBC has found its.' We cannot afford to wait for the BBC to find itself, rather we must compel it to lose control.

The BBC is based upon centralisation and censorship, built upon complete control of the primary channels of culture and communication in a heterogeneous society which belies the homogeneous image of that church whose mission is to create the illusion of unity where none exists in practical terms. Amending the gospel and clearing the vision of the BBC will not render our society any more free than it is at present. A programme to reform the BBC merely locates the political problems of its society in the personal decisions of its hierarchy or, to be much more specific, any plan to reform the BBC which takes as its starting point the postulation or the assumption that our society is free and democratic is destined to succumb to a morass of contradictions. An organisation as undemocratic as the BBC is a precise indicator of the absence of freedom in our society and its reformation would militate against the extension of liberty by emphasising the freedom of institutions at the expense of the institution of freedom. The 'haughtiness' of the BBC is not a temporary fault but a perennial political dilemma. How can any institution in a capitalist society function as a free agent? This is no time for reverence, revelations, reformation or apocalyptic tones. It is time for heresy. There is much more at stake than the liberty of the BBC.

Public service broadcasting and the public interest

I

'There could be no question about our supporting the Government in general... Since the BBC was a national institution, and since the Government in this crisis was acting for the people... the BBC was for the Government in the crisis too.' Reith's 'appalling frankness' was always one of his most endearing qualities. But it was often left to others to reap the consequences. His apparent equation, at the time of the General Strike of 1926, of 'government' and 'the people', and of 'a national institution' with a government ministry, has remained to haunt his successors. Even if it proved possible – thanks largely to the licence fee – to resist the identification of the BBC with a department of State, there persisted the vexing association of 'public service' with service to the State seen as the embodiment of the national or public interest. For 'state' read 'nation', for 'nation' read 'public'. The BBC was a public service institution. How could it discharge that duty without falling into the embrace of the State, i.e. the government of the day?

It might be possible for royalty (though only since Victoria). The Church of England, too, could maintain an arm's length distance, though not always and not unequivocally. Both these institutions were old and could command diverse loyalties. The BBC was a new body. Incorporation by Royal Charter rather than Parliamentary statute might confer an antique-seeming dignity, but – as universities are also finding today – it could not disguise the enormous power retained by the government. The issue of the licence to broadcast, the appointment of governors, the level of the licence fee, the right to veto the broadcast of any programme and to insist on the broadcast of any message of its own: all these powers lay with any and all governments. As Reith admitted at the time of the General Strike, the government had a legal and not simply a *de facto* right to commandeer the BBC when it deemed it necessary. The road to 1984 and the Ministry of Truth seemed, if not wide open, at least largely contingent on government purposes and practice.

The early BBC dealt with the problem by avoiding it. Reith despised politics and politicians, and sought to maintain the BBC's independence by ignoring the contentious and, to him, sterile realm of political debate. It did not seem very important to him that, under pressure from the Foreign Office in 1934, Vernon Bartlett's contract was not renewed and his controversial talks on foreign affairs stopped. Nor that the party leaders should throughout the 1930s dictate which politicians should appear on the air – which meant denying the microphone to Winston Churchill, among others. This left the BBC free to get on with what Reith considered the important talks: building it up as a cultural church. Politics did not matter: philosophy, religion, music, poetry and drama – laced with 'light entertainment' as ground-bait – did.

Political issues could not, however, be ignored forever. [Since the Second World War the BBC has increasingly moved into the arena of political discussion and comment, and has, on a number of occasions, come up against the force of government disapproval and attempted direction.] Emboldened by the prestige it acquired during the Second World War as the symbol of the national struggle against tyranny and lies, it has been able to fend off the politicians on several notable occasions. It stood firm against Eden at the time of Suez. It defended its staff against Wilson's wrath over *Yesterday's Men*. It defied Whitehall and Stormont over *The Question of Ulster*. Yet these conflicts settled nothing, and in the summer of 1985 an avalanche of embarrassing cases descended on the BBC. The direct, though informal, approach by the Home Secretary to the BBC governors led to the cancellation of the *Real Lives* programme on Northern Ireland. It was revealed that routine MI5 vetting of BBC journalists and of senior appointments and promotions had been in practice since 1937. There was evidence of the use of the BBC's premises at Bush House by Special Branch police to photography marchers at political demonstrations.

Although an amended version of the *Real Lives* programme was shown later, and the BBC's management announced an end to MI5 vetting (except in certain 'sensitive' areas), the damage had undoubtedly been done. The cumulative effect of these episodes has been to give a sinister meaning not just to the World Service, with its licensed duty 'to plan and prepare its programmes in the national interest', but to the BBC as a whole.

The timing could not have been worse. More than ever before, the future of public service broadcasting turns on the condition of the BBC. Its precarious situation highlights the crisis of public service broadcasting generally. The BBC, by common agreement, symbolises public service broadcasting in Britain. ITV's public service function is founded on and mirrors that of the BBC. It has been so from the start, and the addition of Channel 4, described almost casually at the outset by its Chief Executive Jeremy Isaacs as a 'public service network', confirms this. The present system of 'two State-owned networks' – the phrase is Sir Gerald Beadle's, a former Director of BBC Television – originates in the prior existence of a powerful and respected public service corporation, the BBC. Its continuance depends on the same condition. The BBC is the original, ITV the copy. It is difficult to imagine that, without a BBC capable of discharging its public service function fully and effectively, ITV could or would long continue to do so for its part. Without the BBC as example and necessary point of reference, ITV would succumb to irresistible commercial pressures. If the BBC were to lose credibility, if it were to be seriously weakened by too little money or

Notion of quality threshold.
(cf. Euro argument)

too close an identification with the State, the natural co
for ITV would be to cut and run in the direction of out-and-
out commercialism, on the American pattern. The BBC is
the anchor which prevents this wayward drift out to the seas
of commerce.

The BBC's predicament, therefore, is also ITV's, insofar
as it sees itself as a partner in the public service duopoly of
British broadcasting. But the duopoly is not really one of
equal partners. ITV needs the BBC for survival as a public
service body at all. The BBC merely needs ITV to stop itself
from becoming pompous and complacent. All the more
reason that the BBC should define, as clearly as it can, its
role as a national institution operating in the public interest.
What is its relation to the public, and to the national culture
as a whole? How has it seen its public service function, and
how far it is able to carry it out?

It is an irony, fraught with consequences for the BBC's
sense of its role, that the period in which it rose to national
prominence was also the period in which its relation to the
mass public was at its most marginal. This fact, obvious as
soon as one reflects on the early BBC's relationship with
British society, is curiously hidden by the standard institutional histories of the BBC as well as by its own received
wisdom of its past. According to the familiar story, Reith
by the time of his departure in 1938 had built up a national
institution of formidable prestige and authority. Contem-
poraries played their part in forming this account. 'You have
created,' Sir Maurice Hankey wrote to Reith on his retire-
ment from the Director-Generalship, 'one of the greatest
organisations in the world, which will continue on your lines
for centuries.' Newspapers congratulated Reith on having
made the BBC as typical and representative a national institution as the Bank of England: reliable and responsible, the
safe depository of the nation's cultural capital.

There is obviously some truth in this account, at the level
at least of national and BBC ideology. The BBC had become
well-known, and its position well enough established to be

the subject of public debate and occasional controversy. But the very speed with which this entrenchment is supposed to have taken place – less than a dozen years since the BBC's incorporation as a public body – should make us suspicious of the more extravagant claims for the centrality of the BBC in the nation's life. The analogies with the Bank of England, Parliament and the Church of England may be suggestive for certain purposes but they should not mislead us into exaggerating the range or depth of the BBC's engagement with British society. Whatever its aspirations at the time, the BBC could hardly be said to be speaking for Britain, still less *to* it. Its relative newness, its conception of its role as the guardian of high culture and morality, its self-denying ordinances against dealing with 'controversial' matters, all militated against a true involvement with the deeper and more varied levels of the society.

The evidence suggests that, on the eve of the Second World War, the BBC itself was becoming uneasily conscious of this lack of engagement. From sources as diverse as Charles Siepmann's report from the Regions in 1936 and its own Listener Research (started in the same year), it learned that it was failing to reach large sections of the people, or, at any rate, failing to make them feel that it had much to say to them. This is hardly surprising considering that as late as 1938 the Music Department – which dealt only with classical and 'light classical' music – alone supplied over fifty per cent of the total output of the National Programme. One can at least understand the groans of the South Wales families that, according to a *Listener* survey of 1938, greeted the news that there were to be seven Toscanini concerts broadcast in the month of May. Moreover, the BBC knew what, for most of the 1930's, the consequences of this policy were. Listeners deserted the BBC and turned to the foreign commercial stations, such as Radio Normandie and Radio Luxembourg – especially on the Reithian Sunday, when one out of two British listeners switched to Luxembourg. Inevitably it was the working-class audience – a quarter of whom were said to listen regularly to foreign stations and two-thirds on Sundays – and working class regions – the North East, South Wales, and the London area – which felt most alienated from the BBC. But many middle class listeners also showed themselves unhappy with the BBC's devotion to virtue and the life of the mind. Listener Research revealed, somewhat to the consternation of programme-makers, that people of all classes and educational backgrounds looked to radio largely for relaxation and entertainment. Only at times of the big national events – a coronation, a Cup Final, a test match, a declaration of war – did radio really appear to speak to an attentive national audience.

Peter Eckersley, one of the co-founders of the BBC, attributed the BBC's remoteness from its audience in the interwar years to its anxiety to achieve legitimacy and respectability in the eyes of the 'powers-that-be': the politicians especially, but also the cultural intelligentsia. The BBC, he wrote in 1941, 'overconcentrated upon securing its foundations' and 'this prevented any clear conception of what was to be built upon them'. The BBC's own practices and policies are clearly one part of the story. But it is fair to say that it probably would not have mattered very much what the BBC had tried to do. Whoring after the gods of variety and vaudeville, in the manner of Normandie and Luxembourg, would simply have added the opprobrium of a bad name to the indifference of the public. The pursuit of popularity in these terms was irrelevant. The difficulties faced by the BBC in the pre-war period were of a far more general and intractable kind. They had to do with the nature of British society as such, and the whole problem of a national institution seeking to penetrate into the daily lives of diverse communities, many of which were still tightly-knit and resistant to mass centralised pressure.

These difficulties faced other national institutions. But Parliament, for instance, was not particularly interested in making direct contact with the electorate, least of all on a day-to-day basis. So long as the electors turned out to vote at regular intervals, it was in fact preferable that they should remain passive at other times, and leave the management of affairs they could not possibly understand in the hands of their elected representatives. Much as it might like it, such an attitude could not so readily be adopted by the Church of England, with its acknowledged concern for the state of its members' souls, and repeated attempts were made to put the Church into closer touch with the lives of ordinary people. But while the failure of these efforts might weaken the Church's authority and influence, it did not really threaten its institutional existence. As with the colleges of Oxford and Cambridge, age and wealth were enough to sustain it through the lean times.

What was unique about the BBC's mission, as Reith conceived it, was not simply that the instrument, the national broadcasting institution, was so raw and so recent, and so hedged round with dangers that it might be stifled in its infancy. It was that, unlike politics and religion, broadcasting, as a medium of unique immediacy with the power to enter directly into the home of every citizen, could only succeed by mobilising the mass of its listeners on a constant, everyday basis. It was a cultural agency of an entirely new kind. It worked, not by passionate appeal at the election hustings, nor by the weekly sermon as in church, but by a day-to-day, hour-by-hour, sometimes minute-by-minute diet of speech and music and the most varied kind. Although the special, spectacular, national broadcasting event could be uniquely powerful as an integrating force, it was not of the essence of the new medium. The keynotes were frequency and continuity, a round-the-clock relationship between broadcaster and listener. Broadcasting's effect depended essentially on there being no real competitor for the time and attention of its audience. Only when broadcasting could achieve a virtual monopoly of its audience's time and interest might an organisation like the BBC even hope, as Reith did, to use the 'brute force' of its own monopoly 'to instruct and fashion public opinion, to banish ignorance and misery, to contribute richly and in many ways to the sum total of human well-being'.

Such a condition, to an extent that would have startled and probably alarmed the broadcasters of the 1930s, was actually attained in later years. In the 1930s and 1940s, with the possible exception of the war years, it remained remote from the experience of the vast majority of people in Britain. Radio was popular, but so too were rival claimants on leisure time – sport, the cinema, pubs and dance halls. Newspapers still provided the bulk of news and comment for all classes in society. People worked longer hours and holidays were fewer, so limiting leisure time. Even the unemployed in the 1930s, unlike today's unemployed, did not spend much time listening to the radio but hung around the streets and cadged drinks in pubs. Most important of all, we are apt to forget how slowly the process of cultural – as opposed to political and economic – centralisation has worked in this country. Newspapers were national, it is true, but provincial newspapers remained strong, and the everyday life of many communities were still tied to a pattern not very dissimilar to that of Victorian and Edwardian times. This was especially true of working class communities, as both Priestley's *English Journey* and Orwell's *Road to Wigan Pier* indicated in their different ways. The future belonged to broadcasting; but radio in this period had to reckon with the persistence and resilience of cultural forces infinitely stronger than anything it was capable of mustering, despite the glamour and evident appeal of the new medium.

The cultural autonomy and diversity of the regions, so marked a feature of nineteenth-century Britain, were certainly being eroded in the first half of the twentieth century. Broadcasting, by being established from the first as a centralised monopoly, made its own contribution to this development. But it took the Second World War and its aftermath to hasten this process decisively. Up until then the BBC's assumption of a 'national community' which it could address directly from Broadcasting House in London was premature, and gave it a misleading sense of its influence. The *BBC Yearbook* for 1933 asserted the principle that 'broadcasting should be operated on a national scale, for national service and by a single national authority'. Only the last of these could truly be said to be operative at this time. Ironically it was in this very period that Reith, with few dissenting voices among his staff, was impatiently closing down local radio and replacing it with the Regions. Local radio, though in existence only for a few years, had been a success. It had established relationships between broadcasters and local audiences which were only rarely to be achieved in a later age of local radio. The Regions by contrast were a technical and administrative convenience with no real cultural significance. As Cleghorn Thompson put it in 1937, their work largely consisted of 'a skilful process of chink-filling applied to a structure devised and dictated from London'. Reith was opposed to the encouragement of 'sectional' interests and loyalties. The Regions remained in the shadow of London, the servants of the search for that elusive mass national audience whose 'general needs' British broadcasting aspired to serve in the public interest.

The mass national audience has now more or less come into being; but the BBC had lost something of the boldness of its pioneers who sought to serve its public by giving it, not what it wanted, or thought it wanted, but what was considered good for it. At the very time when the Reithian goal has become practically possible, public service broadcasting has been in retreat from it.

It is ironic, again, that this process should have started during the Second World War: in the very period, that is, when the BBC is generally held to have reached the acme of its national standing, to have made itself almost synonymous with Britain (if not quite the British). This could have been the springboard for developing that relationship between the national institution and its mass public that Reith had desired, but failed to achieve for reasons largely outside his control. Instead, the BBC took fright from the findings of its Listener Research department before and during the war. The popularity of the programmes of light entertainment on the Forces Programme – which immediately took seventy per cent of all listeners – was seen as the portent of the way things must be in the future. The BBC must follow at least as much as, perhaps more than, it led its public. After the war it divided itself up into Home, Light, and Third Programmes, each more or less tailored to different levels of brow. The Director-General, Sir William Haley, still clung to the hope that this structure would operate as a 'cultural pyramid', leading the listener gradually from 'good to better'. Reith on the other hand saw the Third Programme as 'a sop to moral conscience', an admission that overall programme policy had been abandoned.

The future was to prove Reith the better prophet. In the late 1960s the whole notion of 'mixed programming' – the keystone of Reith's strategy – was given up as radio fragmented further into Radios 1, 2, 3, and 4. Local radio, both BBC and commercial, added to the many layers and levels. Meanwhile the BBC's claim to speak exclusively for and to the nation was severely knocked by the arrival of another broadcasting organisation, ITV, equally anxious to show itself a servant of the public interest. As television in its turn diversified into four channels, the task of identifying and addressing a national audience became surprising difficult. Broadcasting seemed to be following the supermarket principle. It offered a variety of wares matched to the social and cultural profiles of a plurality of potential audiences. As with the supermarket, the choice was in theory left to the consumer. But the broadcasters had all the instruments of market research at their fingertips to direct their goods where they knew they would be as welcome as a familiar and comfortable set of old clothes. The cultural pyramid, far from ascending as Haley had hoped, seemed to be rapidly collapsing into its base.

The paradox of all this is that the fragmentation of national broadcasting has occurred at the very time when a national culture of broadcasting has become both more urgently needed and more practicable. Both the need and the practicability spring from the same social phenomenon: the disintegration of traditional cultures and communities in the postwar period. What Hitler's bombs began, 'urban redevelopment' after the war continued even more effectively. So too did other social changes associated with the decline of old industries, population migrations to the areas of the new industries, especially the motor industry of the Midlands and the service industries of the South, the influx of new immigrants from overseas, and the rise of new towns and 'urban villages' in the countryside. These changes hardly added up to a 'classless society', despite certain claims in the 1950s and 1960s. But they did mean the emergence of new social configurations seeking definition in the national culture: whether those on the large housing estates ringing the older towns and cities; the new youth groups brought into being by post-war prosperity; the new ethnic groups; or the 'new working class' of affluent manual workers and the 'new middle class' of not so affluent white-collar workers.

The older cultural agencies were incapable of supplying these new groups with the necessary cultural bearings. The cinema was in steep decline, newspapers had become largely feature magazines or comic sheets, politicians and churchmen largely the material for television satire. For their part the new groups, unlike the old, were the leading expression of a process of fragmentation and privatisation that has been one of the outstanding features of recent British society. Work or employment, whether available or not, has receded in significance in the lives of the majority of the population. All interest and energy, and increasing amounts of time, have gone into the home. The home is now a small power-plant of domestic capital equipment by means of which households deliver a good part of 'final' goods and services, from clean clothes to private transport. Leisure, above all, has become dominated by home-based equipment and activities. A 1985 survey found that the average British family was spending nearly £2,000 a year on leisure pursuits in the home. Most of these centre on television.

Broadcasting, especially television, was ideally suited to fill the gap left by other cultural agencies. As a medium it is better equipped than any other to speak directly to the privatised household group. It is the mass medium *par excellence,* depending for its power on the centralised source and the dispersed privatised, mass audience. The rise of pressure groups for women, blacks, old people and others, has given an entirely spurious impression of heterogeneity to the mass audience in Britain. By comparison with the differences that marked regions, classes and communities in the last century and even in the first half of this, the most conspicuous feature of the contemporary British public is its essential homogeneity of culture. The mass national audience, announced so often since Tocqueville and Mill and assumed too quickly by Reith and the early B B C, finally arrived in Britain in the decades after the war. Television, as the most socially representative of all the media, indeed as the most socially representative British institution *tout court,* both reflects and reinforces this.

This gives broadcasting both its opportunity and its responsibility. The fragmentation of society allows it to reach a vast and receptive audience. It has done so spectacularly. However we finally assess it, a television viewing-time average of thirty to thirty-five hours a week remains remarkable. It is, however, precisely because of the range and depth of its penetration that broadcasting has to conceive of itself primarily in public service terms. It can do what no other national institution can do. Neither education, religion, royalty, nor politics seem capable of providing that sense of participation in a national culture that a socially fragmented society requires. Although this is hardly the place to talk sociology, it is difficult not to recall here Durkheim's insistence that the pluralism of modern societies was not in itself a principle of integration. Without some overarching sense of cultural purpose, without a cultural framework within which the separate parts could find definition and meaning, industrial societies would lose themselves in conflict and anomaly. Religion had previously provided that cultural skin. Durkheim hoped that, in its place, education might. It is obvious now that he was wrong. By the default of other possible agencies, the task has fallen to broadcasting.

It is important to be clear about what we mean by a national broadcasting culture. It should not mean – to repeat an earlier point – simply that certain national events are made available to a national audience. The Hunt Report on cable expansion, while generally taking a permissive view, nevertheless thought it right that 'the great national events should continue to be protected for the sake of the average viewer who has been used to seeing them on broadcast television'. It showed particular solicitude for 'the FA Cup Final, Wimbledon, Test Matches, the Derby, the Grand National, the Oxford and Cambridge Boat Race and the Commonwealth Games when held in the United Kingdom' (paras. 69-70). T. S. Eliot, in a similarly restrictive list of components of the national culture, shared this obsession with sport but at least also included 'Wensleydale cheese, boiled cabbage cut into sections, beetroot in vinegar, nineteenth century Gothic churches and the music of Elgar'. No doubt such listings are not to be taken too seriously, but they illustrate the dangers of conceiving public service broacasting in terms of special events or issues of national importance. As Eliot conceded, 'every reader can make his own list' – and one would not want to depend on a list drawn up by the politicians. Public service broadcasting has to follow the intimations of the medium itself in providing a daily service that is continuously and throughout infused with a sense of its public function. This need not mean a sequence of relentlessly high-minded programmes. It is a conception that should embrace television Shakespeare and Waugh, *Not the Nine O'Clock News* and *Minder*, *Weekend World* and *Newsnight*, the varied output of Radio 4 and of Channel 4. It should understand and seriously entertain its editor's claim that *Blue*

Peter is 'archetypal public service broadcasting'.

Without such breadth public service broadcasting can become elitist and authoritarian. But this is not the same thing as the unseemly transatlantic pursuit of *Dallas* and *Dynasty,* and the cramming of the schedules with quiz-shows and celebrity chat shows. This shows a contempt for the audience, not simply as it is but also as it might be, that must make one wonder whether public service broadcasting is currently in secure hands. Asa Briggs makes the point that 'Reith's theory of public service began with a conception of the public. Without such a conception the conception of public service itself becomes bleak and arid'. Reith may have erred somewhat on the side of high-mindedness, and showed too uncompromising a distaste for Listener Research, but he never lost his respect for his audience. He had the idea, as Anthony Smith puts it, 'of serving a public by forcing it to confront the frontiers of its own taste'. Briggs says that Reith never talked of 'the mass' or 'the mass media'. He spoke of 'the public', or a series of 'publics' which together constitute 'the great audience'. 'The "publics" are treated with respect not as nameless aggregates with statistically measurable preferences, "targets" for the programme sponsor, but as living audiences capable of growth and development.' In the same spirit, the former Managing Director of BBC Radio, Howard Newby, has also suggested an attractive conception of the national audience that recognises both its unity and its differences, its capacity to produce a 'national response' as well as to pursue various and separate interests. Serving particular minority interests does not, however, subvert the overall national concern 'because of the way audiences. . . overlap with other audiences and so make up a national response which is at a deeper and more satisfying level than would be the case if the broadcasters were trying to maximise their audiences all the time'. The relationship between mass and minority is reciprocal, and depends for its proper working on the existence of a large independent organisation. 'Only a large popular organisation can have a relationship with the whole of society and not just parts of it. The knowledge of such a relationship is necessary for the assurance that makes genuine minority broadcasting possible. . .' There is a very real sense in which philosophers talk on Radio 3 because Morecambe and Wise appear on Radio 2 and on BBC television.

At some point in the future, fibre-optic cable and direct broadcasting by satellite are going to offer a strong challenge to the possibility of this kind of relationship between the national broadcasting organisations and their public. Broadcasting Babel will be at hand, bringing with it the prospect of the complete fragmentation of audiences. Some, like Peter Jay, will welcome the arrival of 'electronic publishing', and will call for the dismantling of the IBA and the disestablishment of the BBC. If the argument of this essay is correct, such an outcome would be disastrous. Whatever increase in consumer choice might ensue – and it is by no means clear that this would be the case – would be more than offset by the collapse of a national system and culture of broadcasting, whose survival is a requirement of the culture as a whole.

Others, like Christopher Dunkley, will say that the BBC cried wolf with the coming of commercial television in the 1950s, and that there is no more reason now to heed the strident and self-interested warnings of the duopoly that the new media technologies will destroy public service broadcasting. Whether or not this optimism proves justified, there can be no doubt that the national broadcasting organisations will have to fight to maintain themselves in anything like their present position. The record of the past thirty years will provide them with some claim on public loyalty and support. But they will need in the meantime to show that they deserve the continued support of the public. They will find it difficult to do so if they appear too timid or too susceptible to government opinion, as seems to have been the case recently not just with the BBC but also the IBA. Equally the present tendencies towards chasing the audience, at the cost of attempting to educate or elevate it, are bound

to make many feel that a fully commercialised broadcasting
system may not be so very different from what seems currently on offer under the present system. The BBC needs to
resist advertising, certainly, even if this means cutting down
on some of its operations. To have to compete with ITV for
advertising, even if there is more of it than at present, will
as irretrievably change its character as it would undoubtedly
drive ITV fully into the arms of commerce. But the BBC will
find few to regret that change if, under the pressure to gain
popularity, it sets itself on this path of its own accord.

In the end, one does have to come to the slightly unex-
pected conclusion that public service broadcasting is too
important to be left to the broadcasters. In a society in which
the parts find it almost impossible to relate directly to each
other or to the whole, a broadcasting system which can provide a national frame of reference has a paramount role to
play. But it is neither to the politicians, nor to the advertisers
and their clients, that we can look to ensure that the broadcasters perform this role adequately. Both of the former
groups have their own axes to grind, while the broadcasters,
for their part, might very well plump for survival on any
terms (as the universities seem hell-bent on doing). There
remains another interested party: large, unorganised and
inclined to be fairly inactive – the broadcasting audience
itself, the public. It is to the continuing vigilance and scrutiny
of the public that we have to look for the maintenance of
public service broadcasting. In Reith's time, public service
broadcasting sought a public that was either uninterested or
unavailable. Now the public has to see that public service
broadcasting keeps faith with its own original ideals.

chapter 5   CHARLES JONSCHER

The economics and technology of television financing

There are essentially three different ways in which television can be – and at least in some countries is – financed: through commercials, through compulsory fees payable irrespective of viewing habits, and through subscriptions payable in accordance with the channels or programmes viewed. There are variations on each of these basic themes. Commercial support can take the direct form of product advertising or have the low profile of programme sponsorship. Government-mandated fees can be levied on television owners, as in the case of the BBC licence, or on the tax-paying population as a whole, as in the case of the public broadcasting service in the USA. A direct viewing charge can be made either for a whole channel (typically on a monthly basis) or for individual programmes such as films and sporting events. These differences of detail may be significant; sponsorship may be less obtrusive than direct advertising; it may be argued whether tax status or television ownership is a more equitable basis on which to determine a citizen's contribution to publicly-funded television (and the licence fee mechanism may provide more insulation from treasury pressure); direct charges may be commercially more viable on a per channel or per programme basis. Despite these variations essentially three different principles of funding can be identified: either the consumers pay through higher prices of goods and services promoted through the television channel, they pay a flat rate agreed by political consensus, or they pay for what they wish to see in more or less the same way as they would for most other goods or services.

After decades of reliance on the second of these methods – compulsory payments – as the means of financing the BBC, the British government is contemplating a shift towards some other method of funding. Since the technology for effecting the third method is not yet available on a universal basis, the most obvious candidate for the supplementing or replacement of the present source of BBC funding is the first option – commercial support through advertising or sponsorship. The purpose of this chapter is to review some of the economic principles which underlie television financing, and to show how developments in the technology of broadcasting will affect the relative merits of the different financing mechanisms.

The first question I would like to pose is whether there is an intellectually sound justification for not giving the market – the free forces of competition and commerce – exclusive power to determine the quality and quantity of programming provided to the public. Until technologies for effecting direct payment for service (to be discussed later in this chapter) are widely available, free market funding of television means advertising funding. Before beginning to answer this we should recognise that the role of television in society can be viewed in two quite different ways. The first is as an important influence on the cultural, social and political life of a country, having many impacts too subtle and diffuse to be adequately handled by the mechanical forces of the market. The second is as a purely economic commodity, an entertainment service whose value should be measured, like that of any other commodity, in terms of willingness to pay by its consumers. It is perhaps not surprising that, when television is viewed in the former role, many arguments have been made for government-controlled funding or other forms of intervention in the market. I will not attempt to comment on these issues here. What is perhaps more suprising is that a case can be made against relying exclusively on commercial funding even when television is viewed purely in its role as an economic commodity.

The reason is that commercial advertising, as a means of raising revenue for television channels, exhibits a quite striking market failure. The term 'market failure' is used to describe a situation in which a market does not fulfil correctly its function of efficiently allocating resources to the production of economic goods and services in relation to the desires of consumers. In a well-functioning market the consumers on the buying side can signal, through their purchasing power, to the producers on the selling side what level of supply of a good or service should be provided, and also what variety of attributes or diversity of quality the goods provided to the market should exhibit. If television were paid for by consumers directly on the basis of programmes watched (without the need for cumbersome or expensive technology), the same might be true of the market for broadcasting. As with any consumer or industrial market, some buyers would be willing to pay more for high quality while others would prefer to pay less for lower quality; the market would supply a variety of programmes to suit these different tastes. If, however, the method of payment is through advertising, there is a problem: the willingness of advertisers to pay for a commercial slot is clearly not proportional to how much viewers are enjoying the programme which is interrupted. Unlike in conventional markets, the revenue collected is proportional only to the number of viewers watching the programme, not to their level of appreciation of it. The result is a strong bias in the allocation of resources to programme production – a bias in favour of programmes which a lot of people like a little and away from programmes which a few people like a lot. Unlike the market for cars, food or furniture, in which consumers can vote (with their pound notes) for quality, diversity or originality as well as quantity, in the market for advertising-supported television consumers can only vote for quantity. The tendency for television, in countries which rely exclusively on competitive commercial markets for programme support, to produce uniform programming which fails to cater for special needs is well-known and provides empirical support for this simple theoretical assertion.

If the first failure of the advertising market is to produce a bias against quality and variety in television production, the second, a perhaps more important failure, is its tendency to under-allocate resources to the industry. This second element of market failure is more difficult than the first to establish on the basis of economic principles or theory, but if true it is particularly serious. The requirement that a competitive market should allocate the correct total volume of resources to the production of a given category of goods or services is even more fundamental to the operation of a capitalist system than the requirement to match consumers' tastes for quality. The argument here is simply that it is a particularly ineffective way to charge for a service to withdraw it periodically and substitute something else – specifically, to substitute an exhortation to purchase a quite unrelated product. The oddness and inefficiency of this method of effecting the necessary signals from the buying side of the market to the producing side – as to the total financial resources which should be committed to producing television programming – can be highlighted by contemplating how such a method would operate if it were applied to any other market. Normally when consumers buy products for their enjoyment, say, items of garden furniture, they expect to pay a price related to the satisfaction they will derive from the purchase, and then to benefit from the product in the normal way. How would sales of garden chairs fare if, for some reason, it were impossible to charge money for their purchase, and instead revenue had to be raised by implanting in the chairs a mechanism which periodically caused them to cease to provide seating support and instead projected messages financed by local businesses? Not many chairs would be produced or sold, and economists would not pronounce themselves satisfied with the functioning of that market. Yet that is how we finance commercial television.

These arguments imply only that advertising support for television is inadequate, not that it is objectionable. No objection can be raised on the basis of economic principles to advertising supported channels supplementing programming supported by license fees or subscription charges. (No objection, that is, based on consideration of the broadcasting market. Advertising also affects, of course, the markets for the products being advertised. Whether the impact on these is beneficial or adverse is a matter of some controversy. Benefits cited include the informative value of commercials, helping buyers identify sellers of products which could be of use to them, and perhaps more important, the ability of advertising to allow a rapid build-up of demand for new products. The technology of modern industries is such that many products can only be produced efficiently on a very large scale and following a large capital investment. If mass audience advertising outlets were not available, first-year sales of a new product would often not be sufficient to provide a commercial return on this capital, and a less dynamic economy would result. Possible adverse macro-economic effects include the tendency to enhance monopolistic power – typically only the biggest players in a market are able to afford television commercials – and the diversion of household income towards greater consumption expenditures and less investment, which in Europe and America, by contrast with Japan, probably aggravates an already unhealthy shortfall in the latter.)

Do our current mechanisms of television financing – advertising support with the market failure characteristics I have described and a licence fee whose value is subject to intense political pressure – indeed cause too few economic resources to be channelled into television production? (By too few I mean less than consumers would be willing to pay for if they could decide how much entertainment service to purchase in the normal way.) Circumstantial evidence certainly seems to point this way. The revenues raised by the licence fee and advertising income amount to the equivalent of some 40p per day per household. Given the central role that television plays in a typical family's life, and the fact that average viewing time is measured in hours per day, it is difficult to imagine that this 40p is commensurate with the market value of the service. A household typically spends about the same on newspapers and magazines – around 20p on the daily paper and a comparable amount on Sunday editions, second papers, magazines and the like. Yet there is no comparison between the importance of these two media as sources of entertainment. The failure of a morning newspaper to appear on the doorstep due to a strike or a delivery boy's slip-up is regarded as a minor irritant. The failure of all television channels to appear for an evening would be an event of far greater magnitude. Newspapers are not printed on certain Bank Holidays; it is unthinkable that television channels would go off the air on Christmas Day.

Thus in a world in which it does not seem possible to allocate as much financial resource to television production as consumers would be willing to pay for, the compulsory licence fee is justified for the simple reason that it helps redress – at least partially – the shortcomings of the advertising market in this respect.

In the long run salvation must lie, clearly, in the development of technologies which allow a consumer to pay directly for programming. In such a technological world, subscription and advertising-supported channels should satisfy all the programming tastes that consumers are willing to pay for. Public funding, if it has a role at all, would be used to subsidise the production of certain *programmes*, not necessarily entire channels, which were deemed to have particular cultural or civic value. In the rest of this chapter I will consider whether technological change is moving in a direction which will make this possible.

Judging by the intensity of media attention, the technological developments which will do most to revolutionise the television industry in the coming years are broadband cable and satellite. This is a misconception, based on a preoccupation with the idea that the delivery channel is the bottleneck holding up the provision of more and better television services. Indeed neither cable nor satellite are even new technological developments: broadband cable television systems have been in place in some locations for several decades and some communications satellite systems have been operational for over two decades. The bottleneck is not the physical distribution channel but money – the ability to receive from consumers the money they are willing to pay for entertainment, and direct that money through an efficient transaction mechanism to those who produce programmes and create channel schedules. Therefore the technologies which will revolutionise the industry are not transmission systems but processing systems, or to be more specific, systems for processing transactions and money.

Transmission technologies and processing technology have always been the cornerstones of information technology, representing the basis of the telecommunications and computing industry respectively. Processing has been revolutionised by one key device, the large scale integrated circuit or 'chip'. Developments in transmission have been less dependent on a single device; a number of important milestones such as the introduction of satellites and, much more recently, of fibre-optic communications, stand out. (The distinction between processing and transmission technologies is beginning to blur, since many recent advances in telecommunications are due more to the ability to process the signal effectively at each end than to an improvement in the raw transmission medium itself; nevertheless it is still useful to consider them separately.)

The processing device which holds out most hope for improving the efficiency of the television market from a transaction standpoint is the addressable set-top converter. The addressable converter is a microprocessor- (i.e. 'chip') based device which allows the distributor of a television programme to control whether an individual viewer is or is not shown a given programme or channel. Each viewer's television set is 'addressed' by the broadcast television signal, and the set is switched or not switched into the subsequent programme depending on whether the particular household is authorised to receive it. It provides the essential basis for an efficient market to exist; the viewer can indicate whether or not he is willing to pay for a programme or channel, and the seller of programmes is able to provide the programme conditionally on this willingness to pay. The broadcast can reach the home either over the air waves in the conventional manner, via satellite, or through broadband cable networks. The cable networks do not have to be switched or two-way. The transmitted picture must, of course, be scrambled, and one of the functions of the processing devices in the set-top converter is to descramble the signal for those consumers who have elected to pay for it.

During the past decade the cost of both transmission and processing technologies has fallen fast, and, according to most forecasts, these trends are likely to continue in the decade to come. The reduction in cost per unit of stored information of an integrated circuit has amounted to approximately thirty-five per cent per year (compound) over the last fifteen years, corresponding to an 640-fold drop in cost during that time. The fall in cost of transmission systems is difficult to measure because of the diversity of technologies available, but a figure in the region of fifteen to twenty per cent per year would more reasonably represent the fall in cost of communication channels over the same period. Both trends are forecast to continue at a comparable rate over the coming years. This is an additional reason why processing technologies hold out more hope than new transmission channels for television development.

Addressable set-top converters are now being introduced into US cable television networks at a cost to the network operator of some £100 to £150 per set. If this cost fell to an acceptable level, it would be possible to introduce such devices into all UK television sets, and then to scramble the transmissions of the BBC and any other non-advertiser-supported services in order to introduce the new transaction mechanism. Consumers would make, say, quarterly or annual payment to programme-providers who would signal to the converters to maintain service so long as the account is in credit.

At some time in the future , perhaps five years from now, the price of these devices will have fallen to the point where the BBC could scramble its services without presenting the poorer members of the community with an excessive cost barrier if they are to continue obtaining BBC services. The licence fee could then become conditional on the viewer's wish to view BBC programmes. It is difficult not to agree, based on the economic principles outlined earlier in this article, that this would be superior to the current compulsory licence mechanism as a means of financing a mass entertainment service. With such technology in place in the majority of households we would look forward to a much greater variety and quantity of television channels, as a result of the ability of the industry to raise money from consumers in the standard way rather than through the inefficient mechanisms of advertising and the politically difficult mechanism of the licence fee. Advertising-supported channels could, of course, continue to exist in this competitive environment. In this future scenario advanced fibre-optics switched star cable networks and high powered direct broadcast satellite systems may have a role to play but again they may not. As I have said before, transmission systems are not in fact the bottleneck. Very rudimentary one-way cable networks such as have been in place for several decades in the UK would be adequate to support the transmission of several new channels. The scarce resource is not transmission-band width but programme supply.

Addressability to individual subscribers can be achieved through the enhancement of cable systems to incorporate switching and two-way transmission. For this reason the present UK government is encouraging the installation of switched star architecture networks in place of the traditional tree-and-branch systems in the new cable franchise areas. In the very long run interests of developing a nationwide broadband telecommunications infrastructure, this policy may, perhaps, have some justification. As a strategy to encourage the growth of television services it is, however, inappropriate. It focuses on using expensive enhancements to the communications channels rather than inexpensive improvements to the terminals to carry out information processing. A cable system costs in the region of £1,000 per subscriber; set-top converters a small fraction of that. If instead of cabling two million homes the nation were to invest the same money in set-top technology for all twenty million television households, new television channels would have a mass audience from which to earn revenue. The television revolution which new technology is intended to bring about could be with us much sooner, because the real bottleneck – financing – would be alleviated.

Can we be sure that introducing a suitable transaction technology will increase dramatically the total volume of funding available for television production? There is one recent phenomenon which illustrates this strikingly, namely the introduction of video cassette recorder (VCR) units. The VCR is the first technology which allows consumers to pay on a per programme basis for material which they see on their television screen. The units began to be shipped into the country in modest quantities in 1980, since when 7.6

million households (over forty per cent of all television viewing families) have spent typically £300 to £400 each on a VCR to be able to view films. Revenues from tape rental have risen in that time from £80 million per year to £350 million per year. The figure of £350 million compares with an expenditure of only £95 million to see the same material – feature films – in the traditional environment of a cinema.

The VCR phenomenon demonstrates that there is a pent-up demand for viewing popular materials, such as feature films: a demand which is rapidly exploited if a technology emerges which allows them to be viewed conveniently on the television screen. The capital cost of a VCR unit and the additional cost of renting tapes has not deterred a very large proportion of UK households from subscribing to this new medium. This can make us confident that television channels, provided they are entertaining and of good technical quality, will be able to command substantial revenues if financed on a subscription basis. For this reason the BBC need not be afraid of switching to this new technology at such time when the price drops to a sufficiently low level – perhaps in the region of £50 per unit. This, and not commercial advertising, is clearly the correct long run solution to the funding problem. Meanwhile in the few intervening years it would be a great pity to shift the method of financing the BBC away from the (not ideal) one of licence funding to the (manifestly inefficient) one of advertising when the most efficient transaction mechanism of all is – in the context of the timescale of development of this industry – just round the corner.

Coexistence: a survival strategy for public service broadcasting

'No nation can exist half slave and half free', Abraham Lincoln was fond of saying. To my mind, however, broadcasting can tolerate two seemingly incompatible states. It not only can but will. In Britain the coexistence of regulated broadcasting and unregulated narrowcasting is the most likely outcome of the current turmoil about the broadcasting structures. The questions really are: in what proportion will they coexist, and how, as alternative forms of programme increase and the audience splinters, can the public service side of the mix be paid for.

I am not suggesting that public service broadcasting comes in the 'slave' category. I do think, however, that its future would be less uncertain if it relied less on euphemisms. These abound in British broadcasting. 'Independent' television means commercial television; 'community' radio means small or local radio, and has to be invented because what is called 'local' radio is in fact regional radio. So what is public service broadcasting if you strip away the overtones of self-congratulation: It is regulated broadcasting (and 'regulation' is just  another word for 'control'). Public service broadcasting is a service that puts its programmes together according to certain principles or, for example, according to a mandate to 'inform, educate and entertain'. It also carries certain defined rules on how much of each there should be. Public service broadcasting has overseers to see that it keeps to the programme rules. In Britain it also has been controlled in another way – by regulations which restrict the television audience's access to alternative channels or programmes.

This 'control by scarcity' is disappearing. I wonder if anybody will continue to argue that the proliferation of channels can be stopped by regulation. It cannot. Channel 4 has probably been the greatest fragmenter of the audience that Britain is likely to experience this century and its greatest and unsung achievement is in breaking the grip of the BBC and ITV 1 schedules. The remote control button and the video cassette recorder have placed the choice of viewing in the hands of the viewer, although for the past few years the British broadcasting establishment has reassured itself that 'they're only time-shifting'. The audience was, their statistics showed, watching the four channels, which now huddle together under the banner of public service broadcasting (BBC1 and 2; ITV1 and Channel 4); it was just reshuffling the bits.

With, however, the liberalisation of the rules on satellite television reception at the end of May 1985, the floodgates of new television choice opened upon Britain. It was a victory for the Department of Trade and Industry over the Home Office. The DTI wanted to encourage English-language satellite programme services and the manufacture of British dishes. The Home Office (the traditional regulator of broadcasting and now, by extension, of cable television), in its desire to protect cable from disturbance by newer, rival technologies like SMATV, had been fighting against freer reception. The DTI's victory was greater than anyone expected. Anybody who can get planning permission can now put up a dish and watch whatever is floating down from ECS-1, Intelsat V or Gorizont: Sky Channel, Music Box, the Children's Channel and at least one film channel on pay-TV. Another European satellite, the ECS-3, is on its way and the availability of more transponders will bring Ted Turner's channel and at least two Lifestyle channels (one with the rights to the American cable channel, Nashville). In addition,

American evangelists are ready to pay for 'Christian SMATV' to go out to the Baptists and other fundamentalists around Britain. Soon hotels, military bases, blocks of flats, discothéques, holiday camps and remote villages all over Britain will be tuning in to low and medium-powered satellites.

It is happening all over western Europe. Most of the West German states now get Sky Channel as well as two German commercial channels and one French channel. Denmark, which has for a long time restricted its television diet, is about to let satellite television in. King Juan Carlos has a TVRO on his palace in Madrid. Can Balmoral, if not Buckingham Palace, be far behind?

The dilemma this presents authorities who have regulated by scarcity is sad to behold. Every time Mrs Thatcher's government sees a new source of choice in television spring up, it sets up a new authority to control it. We have the Cable Authority, charged with making rules about the amount of advertising and British content on cable before there is much cable to regulate. We have a Satellite Broadcasting Board long before there is any satellite broadcasting in the orthodox Warc-77 sense and when Britain's own unrealistic plans for a made-in-Britain DBS have collapsed. Lord Whitelaw has even proposed a new local radio authority to regulate 'community radio', which has not yet begun. Even video has not escaped a new authority. The Board of Film Censors has now been given new powers to censor not only film but video; in other words, in order to control 'video nasties', Britain has for the first time acquired an official film censor backed by statutory, not voluntary, powers. None of these authorities will, however, be able to do what is fondly expected of them because there is too much new choice. It is a case of closing the doors when they're coming in through the windows.

So, the only answer to how public service broadcasting can be protected is to make sure that people choose to watch it. It will have to accept that its share of the national viewing audience will drop (the BBC will never have a larger share than the 40 per cent plus it enjoys today), but I believe that people will continue to watch the BBC and ITV channels because their programmes are good, because they like a rich and varied choice, and because they give a sense of national cohesion: when a wall collapses on football fans in Brussels, people are not going to tune into Sky Channel.

The above reasons may attract viewers, but they do not solve the problem of how to pay for excellence if the audience share drops. My own answer is to preserve the present system of finance: a licence fee for the BBC and a monoply on over-the-air television advertising for each commercial television company in the region (or the slice of air time allowed it); *but* then to let the 'new media' go entirely unregulated (apart from frequency regulation), as is appropriate for retail services, or 'transactional services' as Anthony Smith calls them.

The Thatcher government does not like this solution. It is approaching the future of broadcasting from exactly the opposite direction. Not content with trying to regulate all the new media as it appears, it has set up machinery like the Peacock Committee to see if it can shuffle some of the advertising income for ITV over to the BBC, thus taking the part of the broadcasting structure that is known to work and considering whether is should be assembled in another way. To Mrs Thatcher I would quote the American commandment, 'If it's not broke, don't fix it'.

The Peacock Committee is, however, with us, and we will have to play a numbers game. How deep is the untapped pool of advertising? To what extent will advertising on the BBC hurt local newspapers? Will this be more or less than the advertising revenue and circulation already diverted by those increasingly glossy free-sheets (give-away newspapers)? The figures produced will be as significant as those, in the 1920s, about the harm that would be done to the newspapers by the BBC, or, in the 1960s, about the harm that would be done to the British local press by the advent of commercial local radio. I have yet to see any figures which are not self-serving. Of course ITV companies like Granada can produce statistics to show how many radio stations will go under if the BBC takes advertising. They would, wouldn't they? How can there be any figures on the 'effect' of an unknowable quantity like advertising on the BBC? There are too many variables: the amount of time given to commercials, the number of products considered acceptable for advertising on television. Even when all the sums have been done, according to pessimistic and optimistic scenarios, there will remain unpredictable quantities like how much advertising the 'sky channels' are going to bring into Britain. The 'licence fee', the BBC's main source of money, is easy to define, but 'advertising', of which commercial television has a supposed monopoly, is not.

Since, however, ITV has had a very rich pasture to itself for a long time, I feel less disposed to sympathise; and its political arguments against having advertising on the BBC (which is that the proposal comes only from the advertising industry, seeking competitive and lower rates) are strong and will help its case. The BBC is in a much weaker position. In its own strategy for survival, I would advise it to concentrate on the distinctive qualities it offers, for example, a commercial-free service, and not on cut-price supermarket slogans like 'Best Bargain in Britain', which is used when campaigning for a rise in the licence fee.

There is so much broadcasting dogma going around British broadcasting: 'each pays the same, each views the same'; 'the excellence of British television depends on no competition for the same sources of revenue'; and so on. The latter may be true but when repeated too often as an operating principle, it sounds complacent and inflexible.

The dogma of not competing for sources of revenue also makes trouble for the BBC. Having swallowed it, the BBC is prevented from saying aloud what seems to me indisputably true: commercials are annoying. To have produced two national channels of quality and interest, and to have kept them free of advertising, is a great cultural achievement.

As an American in Britain, I am passionately in favour of keeping some television channels free of advertising. Instead of inundating us with the figures it is gathering, the BBC should put on an evening of some of Britain's American favourites – *Dallas*, *Taxi* or *Fame*; but show them as they are experienced by the American viewer, shredded by commercial interruptions. It might further sober up Britain's commercial lobby by putting on an evening of American public broadcasting when they are begging for money and auctioning off the station manager's underwear to pull in dollars. Two-thirds of the way through *Staying On*, a film with Trevor Howard and Celia Johnson, and just as the possibility of death lurched into view, WGBH, Boston's public broadcasting station, interrupted the programme for a twenty-minute fund-raising drive.

In his Logie Baird lecture in June, Anthony Smith, with some justification, accused the BBC of going downmarket and trying to do everything. The BBC has made two other serious mistakes, for which it is now paying dearly. One was to argue that the BBC must have approximately a fifty per cent share of the national audience to justify its claim on the licence fee. The memory of the fuss made in the early days of commercial television when people did in fact complain about having to pay for the BBC when they were only watching the 'other side' is still strong. Yet people pay for a lot of things they do not themselves use: State schools, hydrogen bombs, meals-on-wheels, etc. I have never believed that the issues of the licence fee and the audience share need to be linked. The BBC's task now is to convince the public, and the politicians, that it is in the national interest to retain the licence fee (if necessary topped up by advertising), whether or not its share of the national audience drops (and it is going to drop).

I do not think this is an unrealistic proposition. How many

people complained about the recent raising of the licence fee from £46 to £58? How many protest letters were received by MPs? In fact, there were so few of either that they do not bear counting (whereas an upsetting television programme will draw fifty to one hundred telephone calls in an evening). The BBC should use its ingenuity to lift the burden of the fee from those dependent on the social services and on ways of persuading everybody else to pay by instalments or direct debit.

NHK, Japan's public broadcasting organisation, provides the very model of what I think the BBC should be aiming at in its relations with the public. NHK is entirely supported by licence fees yet it coexists in Tokyo with five commercial channels, and with six in Osaka and some other cities. Some of these are vulgar; others, such as NTV, are as high-minded as Granada. NHK gets, I am told, only about twenty-five per cent of the national audience, yet the Japanese pay their licence fee. The reason why there are so few grumbles is because the Japanese public believes NHK's claim that, as the sole public broadcaster in Japan, it upholds the ideals and traditions of Japanese culture. It is seen to do this because it gives its entire second channel over to education even though this channel includes many popular programmes similar to those produced by the BBC, such as one which translates as *Watching with Mama*. NHK's main strength, however, is its news. The NHK morning news show is watched by the whole country. This brings me to the BBC's other big mistake – to let ITV slip under the public broadcasting blanket with it. Unlike NHK, the BBC cannot easily exhibit the difference between its own 'public' and ITV's 'commercial' broadcasting channels.

The licence fee should remain because it acts as a buffer against government, it is seen to give good value for money and it is collectable, if not easily (and almost not at all in Northern Ireland). It will not, of course, give the BBC an income comparable to ITV's, and I would, therefore, support the solution put forward by Justin Dukes of Channel 4: to take an extra slice of levy away from ITV – based on its total revenues, not just its profits – and divert it sideways to the BBC to allow the BBC's income to rise in step with the increased money (if there is any) from advertising. Then I would let the 'new media' slug it out. Let them have forty-five minutes of advertising. Let the Moonies fill their own cable channel. Leave regulation to what can be regulated – the scarce over-the-air channels which reach into every home and for which the national appetite is well-developed. Let the rest scramble for favour. They will win more than the BBC and ITV like, but less than they want.

Not only do I think this should happen but I think it will happen. Public service broadcasting in Britain will survive through coexistence, not because there is no alternative (there will be dozens), but because it is here, because the British public does not like radical change and because it likes the cohesion and excellence of the familiar national channels.

An end to protection

'An end to protection' is a title that has been bestowed on me, whose misleading qualities I want to dispose of from the start.

There *is* no deregulated broadcasting system anywhere, because the scarcity of frequencies requires governments to decide on their allocation. What I am in favour of is a *less* regulated system than the one we now have in Britain, 'de-regulation' with a hyphen, rather than 'deregulation' with its deceptive suggestion of free-market operation. I want to move towards a system which encourages freedom of speech, diversity and choice, rather than one which serves to protect a series of interlocking interests as its first priority.

The language of that protected system dominates our broadcasting culture. Sometimes it is the crude condescension of a Lord Whitelaw, saying that maybe it was a mistake to allow breakfast television: what has it got to do with him if millions of people want to watch some not very good programmes for thirty hours a week?

A more disingenuous version was expressed to me by a leading columnist on the *New Statesman*: 'by chance, we have a system which provides lots of programmes for cultured, middle-class socialists like me, which is reasonably impartial and fairly cost effective – why are you criticising it?'

And it is cosy for the broadcasters too: witness the bizarre article recently written for *Televisual* by Norman Swallow, doyen of documentary producers. 'Deregulation', he tells us,

'has meant a drop in the standards of British broadcasting
that we have respected for so long' – this before cable has
even a minute audience, before satellites have even begun
transmission! He is quite explicit about 'the danger' from
cable and satellite, indeed from 'any increase in transmission
time, by whatever technical means' – 'the potential effect on
those of us who earn our living and get our job satisfaction,
by making the kind of programmes that even the existing
channels may have to ignore'.

'A bigger threat than any other' would come from a satellite
beaming programmes across the Atlantic. 'An additional
danger' would be a twenty-four-hour news service and soft-
porn (that is Norman Swallow's pairing, not mine). 'So,' he
concludes, 'where do we go from here? By "we" I mean those
of us who earn our livelihood from television and enjoy what
we are able to do.'

I doubt if 'broadcasting for the broadcasters' was what
Richard Francis of the BBC had in mind in his recent lecture
'What is broadcasting for?' Yet, sadly, the presumption that
broadcasting is run by the broadcasters in the best interests
of the public looks increasingly suspect whenever broadcasters denounce as a threat to themselves any prospect of
the viewing public having a chance to choose a new broadcaster's wares.

Orwell would have found a word for it. More (especially
from abroad) means worse, except when it is provided by
the same people who run all the rest of broadcasting, when
more (such as DBS, breakfast television, Channel Four, day-
time programmes, etc.) means better. Indeed, so strong is
the xenophobia built into our broadcasting system that the
BBC's virulent attack on cable television was spearheaded by
the derisive phrase 'wall-to-wall *Dallas*' – *Dallas* being, of
course, the programme transmitted and shamelessly hyped
('who killed JR' made it on to the *Nine O'Clock News*) by the
BBC for years, moved around the schedule to shoot down
potential ITV hits, and the prospect of whose loss to Thames

caused a collective heart attack within B B C management (not to mention costing Bryan Cowgill his job, and exposing British collusive humbug at its worst at the very top of the B B C and I B A) – yes, it was this very *Dallas* which would pollute the airwaves if broadcast on non-B B C-controlled cable. Somehow, 'wall-to-wall *Tenko*' and 'wall-to-wall *Coronation Street*' never quite sprang to the lips of those British broadcasters so keen to see off a potential rival.

It would be a mistake to dismiss the 'wall-to-wall *Dallas*' remark as a slip of the tongue. Deep down, it signifies not just a contempt for foreign programme-makers, but also condescension to the audience. It implies that the B B C transmits *Dallas* cynically as a ratings-puller, not out of any belief in its intrinsic worth. Occasionally, the B B C will attribute the epithet 'quality' to one of its own popular successes (*Fawlty Towers, Last of the Summer Wine*, etc.) but we should not beat about the bush. 'Quality' is overwhelmingly attributed to those middle-class programmes particularly appreciated by the educated elite which controls British broadcasting and British politics. I have no figures at hand, but would guess that, judging by the relative demand in the market place, television over-provides classical music by a factor of ten as compared with pop and rock.

Of course, programme-makers – largely recruited from the educated class – welcome this arrangement and educated foreigners applaud it. The 'historic compromise' further includes workers and trade unions deriving high incomes and security from a stable structure, and, of course, the politicians and madarins who know that they can control or browbeat broadcasters within the regulated system those broadcasters so enthusiastically embrace. As Anthony Smith once put it: 'at the heart of the system lies a promise to politicians as a whole that their specific needs will be catered for.'

One of the puzzles for me, observing this state of affairs, is why the left so rarely criticises it. If books, or magazines, or newspapers, or records, or films or any other form of communication were to be made subject to the kind of regulatory control we suffer in broadcasting, or if foreign material in such areas were to be excluded as a culturally inferior threat, there would be an outcry. Yet, in broadcasting, tight regulation is accepted and applauded. That 'high quality' books, magazines, newspapers, records and films survive and flourish in an unregulated market is no inhibition to the proffered argument that only regulation will preserve 'high quality' (for which, in the main part, read 'highbrow') television.

There is also, of course, for the left the pragmatic view that a slightly muzzled but ostensibly even-handed broadcasting system is better than the flagrant anti-left bias of Fleet Street. But that still does not explain the fierce hostility to cable, which is no conceivable threat to the broadcasting structure. Here I detect a thinly concealed anti-pluralism. When Richard Hoggart delivered his anti-cable piece on *Did You See?*, he harked back to the good old days of shared experience in watching a single television channel as a lost cultural value. And I remember my friend and colleague Phillip Whitehead, twenty years ago, murmuring doubts about the arrival of BBC2, with its Monday-night westerns decimating the audience for *Panorama*. But it is a fatal weakness in a broadcasting philosophy when the desire to improve the audience is allowed to override the duty to provide more choice.

What twenty years in current affairs has taught me is that fragmentation of the audience is to be welcomed, not feared. The more channels there are, the more chance of a current affairs programmes escaping the icy glare of the regulators. Too often we forget the litany of programmes banned outright, cut, postponed or otherwise interfered with by boards and managements at the IBA and BBC. The *World In Action* on Poulson, signals intelligence, Irish republicanism south of the border, aspirin, hunger strikers; *This Week* on Northern Ireland, abortion, corrupt MPs; *Panorama* on MI5, in

Carrickmore; *Twenty/Twenty Vision* on MI5; *The Animals Film; The War Game; The Truth Game;* Michael Collins; *Brimstone and Treacle; Scum; Sex In Our Time; Solid Geometry;* The Legion Hall Bombing; the films shelved during the Falklands war; QED on the effects of nuclear attack, *I Remember Nelson* on the battle of Trafalgar(!). And those are just those that spring immediately to mind, in someone whose memory goes back a little further that *Real Lives*.

Of course, Anthony Smith's John Logie Baird lecture was delivered before the *Real Lives* affair revealed for all to see how vulnerable a regulated broadcasting system is when a strong-willed government and a biddable board of governors coincide – otherwise, he could scarcely have allowed himself to say that the licence fee insulates the BBC from government. Even so, it was depressing to hear such a doughty libertarian offer so uncritical a defence of the broadcasting structure, right down to endorsing the BBC's role as 'the supreme national instrument of broadcasting', a phrase redolent of the 1930s. The jump logic of the corporate mentality was summarised in two sentences: 'All one can say to define the indefinable nature of the BBC is that it is a national institution. To be a great institution it must lead.'

That is all very well as advice to those who aspire to – or find themselves – managing the BBC; but it takes for granted that the licensed, regulated, institutional broadcasting system we live in is the best available. There is a nod in the direction of pluralism, with the warm endorsement of Channel 4 and its involvement of independent producers. But from those of us who advocated from 1972 the precise present structure of Channel 4 – and waited a decade for Anthony Smith to become a convert to it – perhaps a note of caution might temper the enthusiasm.

The 'pluralism' represented by Channel 4 is to add one more middle-aged, middle-class, white, male, Oxbridge graduate to the magic circle of half a dozen or so similar men who decide what is broadcast on British television. That he happens to be the most enlightened broadcasting practitioner known to us is small consolation for the narrowness of the filtering system. As for the independent sector, its fragility is more evident than its vigour. Channel 4 is on record as being committed to a 'stable and secure' independent sector. Yet, in the last year, Channel 4 has reduced total hours of output from the independent sector by 8 per cent, and reduced the average number of hours commissioned from each company by 18 per cent, while at the same time pursuing an explicit policy of forcing down production fees for independents.

In an effort to counteract this trend, some independents have asked the Channel to enter into medium-term arrangements which would allow planning ahead in order to secure continuity of high-class output and a reduction in unit costs. All such proposals have been rejected on the grounds that they would limit Channel 4's flexibility in choosing between ideas offered and companies available. Whether such an attitude constitutes an abuse of Channel 4's monopoly position in the market (in so far as it is exemplified by the deliberate increasing of the number of suppliers and reduction of their profits margins) is a matter open to judgment. What is beyond doubt is that it is in direct conflict with the stated commitment to a 'secure and stable' independent sector.

Even more worrying is the tenuous nature of the arguments deployed by Channel 4. Apparently, to increase from one to two (out of a total of 313) the number of independents with medium-term contracts would threaten the Channel's commitment to innovation. There is also a curious belief that companies able to plan ahead for two years will come up with worse programme ideas than those unable to say if they would even still be in existence three months hence.

The danger in all this is not so much that some suppliers will withdraw to less risky areas – leaving the more marginal operators to compete for Channel 4 contracts – but that programme-makers in search of security will find shelter in facilities companies, in return for guaranteed use of their facilities at no-discount prices when Channel 4 contracts materialise. So the cost advantage independents can generate by picking and choosing among facilities would disappear; and that vertical integration of ideas and hardware which the independent sector was designed to avoid would reappear.

When Channel 4 started, there was much nudging and winking as to which independents would be first on to the USM (Unlisted Stock Market). As it turns out, the level of profit and security is so low for Channel 4 production companies that they are unmarketable. Instead, it is the facilities companies (some, by now, sporting production arms) which have found favour on the USM; after all, even if ideas and producers are regarded as temporary phenomena, the physical means of making programmes will always be in steady demand.

Channel 4 seems little concerned by these developments: its advice to independents is that their long-term security lies in opening up the non-commercial sector of broadcasting (i.e. the BBC). Given that the BBC's initial commitment (yet to be confirmed in practice) is to 150 hours a *year* from independents, the actual increase in total broadcast hours for independents would be 16 per cent – or an average of half an hour per company per annum: scarcely my definition of long-term security. Moreover, the BBC has made it clear that it sees independent productions as to be brought in at about thirty per cent of cost – whereas a good proportion of Channel 4 commissions are 100 per cent funded by the Channel.

There is a separate, much deeper reason for regarding as misguided Anthony Smith's hopes for the BBC to move in the direction of Channel 4's commissioning mode – to become a 'great national foundation' (where have I heard that phrase before?). For the distinguishing feature of the BBC – as opposed to the federal ITV structure – is its central coherence. What makes the BBC valuable is its long-term commitment to drama, current affairs, science, sport, comedy, education and so on – which can only be undertaken on the basis of a large central core of services and staff. There is room for argument as to whether at the margin of its operations the BBC should sustain a fringe of independent productions, whose number could rise or fall according to the BBC's changing needs. But a wholesale switch to Channel-4-style commissioning would mean a monumental upheaval to no discernible benefit. After all, if a second commissioning channel *were* decided on, how much simpler to convert ITV along the lines of the Pilkington report, which recommended that the IBA receive all the advertising revenue and treat the programme companies as suppliers.

Perhaps oddest of all in Anthony Smith's lecture is the side-stepping of the issue of funding of the BBC. The BBC's licence fee dilemma is frankly acknowledged: 'the larger the increase it demands, the more politically vulnerable it renders itself.' The solution is simple: 'operate always within a licence fee that is not excessively politically contentious'! At best, that must mean hoping for inflation-proofing of the licence: but as the 'broadcasting inflation rate' is markedly higher than the RIP (Retail Price Index), the inevitable consequence is a gradual decline in purchasing power. The only way in the past that the BBC has managed to compete financially with ITV has been by its income increasing faster than the index-linking the licence provided for – through the spread of colour licences. That process has halted, which is why the BBC is anxiously casting around for a new form of gearing, such as reviving the radio licence.

To advise the BBC to settle for long-term decline so as to avoid the political fall-out from licence negotiations is the counsel of despair, rooted in the mistaken belief that the licence fee – an inefficient, unfair poll-tax which is slowly strangling the BBC – is 'the most important democratic instrument we possess'. To confuse a rusty mechanism for raising revenue with the financial independence of the BBC is a wholly uncharacteristic misunderstanding, reminiscent of the BBC's own evidence to Annan – that no more direct relationship between broadcaster and audience could be imagined than the licence.

Of *course* there is a more direct relationship: subscription. And of *course* there is a method of funding the BBC which is more democratic and efficient than the licence: subscription. That, after all, is how the BBC was funded for its first thirty years, before the voluntary element (if you want to hear/watch BBC programmes, buy a licence) was overtaken by compulsion (if you want to hear/watch *anyone's* programmes, buy a licence). Two crucial advantages would accrue to the BBC from a reversion to subscription. First, if the BBC was able to argue that it was taking its chances in the market place, it could demand freedom from a government-set licence, and the right to set its own subscription level. Secondly, if subscription operated through a system of scramblers and decoders, a new form of gearing would present itself in the shape of multi-set households and businesses.

The knee-jerk reactions to the idea of subscription have been instructive. 'Discriminatory' – but not if the subscription level were set at the same level as the current licence, and even then only in the sense that *viewers* could discriminate by declining to subscribe. 'Too risky for the BBC' – but only if you assume that large numbers of households are watching ten hours a week of BBC programmes *faute de mieux*, and would gladly give up the 'best bargain in Britain' if they had a choice – in which case, how do we justify forcing people to pay for a television service they would rather do without? 'Inimical to minority programmes' – far from it: the incentive for an across-the-board subscription service is to add on special-interest programmes at the margin, rather than pursue the same majority audience the whole time. 'Too expensive to initiate' – but only if the decoders cost more than £25 each, at which price the BBC could afford to give away twenty million of them to viewers, and recover the money in six years from the elimination of the evasion.

As it happens, the only way the BBC looks like contemplating subscription is as a more efficient form of licence-gathering: scrambling *all* signals, including ITV's, but giving the BBC all the income, including that from multi-set usership. Although it goes against the grain, I would be prepared to concede that compulsory subscription as a first step to true voluntary subscription, as once all the hardware was in place and differential pricing of channels were a practical prospect, the shift to a voluntary system might be more palatable for the BBC itself.

The broadcasting system that might then emerge is a great deal more rational than the one we have at present. All television services – and the present limit of four would quickly give way to a larger number – would set their own level of subscription, judging for themselves what balance to strike between subscriber income and advertising revenue, just as newspapers and magazines do. The regulatory framework could be reduced to the minimum necessary to allocate channels, with all broadcasters subject to simply the laws of the land. Undoubtedly, many broadcasters, if they wish to command the loyalty of subscribers, will continue to operate the various codes of practice they have in the past adopted or had imposed. But the capacity for governmental interference will diminish along with the scarcity of channels and through the abolition of the licence.

In that contect, I think it would be positively healthy for the BBC to be allowed to take advertising if it so wished, and for the ITV tax regime to be overhauled so as to restore normal economic considerations. But the main objective should never be obscured: maximising freedom of speech, through diversity of inputs, multiplicity of outputs and the elimination of all but the most basic of regulations.

Sadly, almost no one working within broadcasting is prepared to put that objective first – the high-cost, restricted-choice, closed and regulated system suits too many people too well – and not just those at the top. And if any mere employees wish to demur publicly, they will quickly find that the 'gag' clause itself is a far worse abuse of freedom of speech and thought than the MI5-vetting affair or the *Real Lives* débâcle: yet the unions which react so fiercely against such blatant abuses have never made a real effort to force the BBC and ITV companies to give their employees the freedom to speak publicly about how broadcasting should be organised. The threat of strike action, used so often to win a percentage point pay increase, could long ago have won such freedom: but within the network of vested interests the system so smoothly serves, that freedom simply does not register.

chapter 8   MARGARET MATHESON
                JEREMY ISAACS
                JOHN CAUGHIE

Co-production in the next decade: towards an international public service

Co-production has a bad name; derived from the notion that it involves too many cooks, each with the ambition to pay less and get more in return.

If the ideal in production finance is to create the appropriate space for a producer (or producing team) to work freely and without interference towards a shared ambition, then the problem with co-financed productions is that all the investors expect their opinions to be heard and the principal investor expects its opinion to be heard most often. Co-production structures too often create a fertile breeding ground for the growth of a disparity of ambitions, when what is wanted is a means of organising the finance without diluting the control of the producer.

The growing prevalence of co-production is not then the result of it being intrinsically desirable; it exists because of opportunity and need. Nor is it anything new; Lew Grade may well have been the godfather of co-finance. He pioneered the UK production of film series (*The Saint, The Persuaders, The Prisoner*) for world use, and did so in direct response to a market opportunity. He later married – with astonishing entrepreneurial skill – Proctor and Gamble, General Motors, RAI, ITV and a US network to make *Jesus of Nazareth*. These programmes delighted audiences around the world, but few would claim that they are notable for their cultural singularity; they were cleverly packaged and well sold.

Until the formation of Euston Films in 1971/2, it was customary for both the BBC and ITV to provide all of their programming from 'in-house'. Since then, however, there has been an increasing need for broadcasters either to finance or to acquire programmes externally because of inflation and the consequent diminishing of internal production funds as well as the unsuitability of both internal facilities and labour agreements for making programmes on film.

The mini-series arrived in force in 1976 with *Rich Man, Poor Man*. UK television had been making serials for some time (in particular, classic serials adapted from books) but the mini-series as understood by US network and cable companies did not concern itself with literary sources but with foreign locations, star casts and, consequently, large budgets. The form of the mini-series has, therefore, laid the basis for the current expansion in co-financing, which has, in turn, provided an opportunity for a growing number of independent companies to produce internationally financed programmes.

The BBC adapted more easily to producing film internally than most ITV companies, with the notable exception of Granada Television. Some ITV companies formed film subsidiaries (for example, Thames, with Euston Films) which allowed them to exploit the fashion for film series in a more cost-effective way than they could have done in-house. But this necessitated real cash investment in programmes and, therefore, real cash returns, hence the logical step to pre-sales and co-finance.

Both the BBC (for in-house production) and ITV (for other film-making subsidiaries) have pursued such co-finance. But now, with the added encouragement of Channel 4 and its commitment to independent production, the most vigorous entrepreneurial activity is to be found outside the broadcast organisations. It should be remembered, however, that the two are interdependent: the desire of producers to work independently marries naturally with broadcasters' financial and editorial needs, and internationally financed projects tend to attract more kudos than 'run-of-the-mill' in-house productions.

The main limitation of co-financed production is, in a sense, its very first step: the original choice of subject. Negotiations about script, casting, swearing, nudity and so on are the producer's stock in trade, but an original and unusual idea may be hard to sell even before any such negotiation stage is reached. The subject is likely to be predictable and safe – bestselling books, historical biography and action adventure series. The BBC has just committed itself to *Impact* (son of *Compact*), a Euro-soap to be jointly financed by Britain, France and Italy about the goings-on in an international magazine office. That a firm decision is reached on a project like this probably has as much to do with the foreign money it could attract as with its content.

Co-venturing, however, may well be more suited to music programmes and documentaries: a Duran Duran concert film is as attractive in the UK and the USA as it is in Italy or France; and *Vietnam, a Television History* was a remarkably successful joint venture involving WGBH (USA), Central (UK) and Antenne Deux (France): a strongly produced venture, with a single editorial voice, which appeared only to benefit from its joint funding. Documentaries have the advantage of a limited market and, since the parameters of that market are clearly defined, there is less incentive to compromise, to subvert the original intention and thus the financial stakes remain relatively low.

It may be useful here to quote a few guide prices. The average cost of one hour of BBC drama is £250,000. The cost of co-financed drama varies enormously, but an internationally sold mini-series such as *The Far Pavilions* or *Kennedy* will cost almost £1,000,000 an hour. For such a mini-series the US network licence fee would now be about $1,200,000 or, alternatively, a US major cable licence is $500,000 to $600,000. The UK purchase price for a blockbuster mini-series would be £100,000 an hour and for a continuing series £35,000 to £50,000 an hour. It is interesting to note that the BBC is currently paying more for its purchased programmes than ITV.

Most co-financing takes the form of a pre-sale which is usually worth more than a sale after completion of the programme. This suits both parties. The pre-buyer is willing to commit early to avoid disappointment later and perhaps to have an involvement in the production, and the producer is unable to finance the programme without the cash in advance. The BBC mainly pre-sells its drama to the USA, Canada and Australia, rather than Europe, where language difference is the prime deterrent.

Genuine co-productions which fall within the framework of international co-production treaties and in which two (or more) parties contribute facilities, labour and expertise as well as funds are less frequent than pre-sales, again because suitable subject matter is hard to find (e.g. an Anglo-something love story, an immigrant or refugee saga, etc.).

The most attractive prospect about co-production from the producer's point of view is the money generated by legitimate tax avoidance. Although financing a production in a benevolent tax climate may involve months of wrangling by bankers and lawyers, it may also leave the producer with investors who have no interest in the production and who, therefore, leave the producer alone to do his/her job with the umbrella of finance, but no interference from financiers. In the UK the pursuit of relief from the ITV Exchequer Levy is almost the only tax-related incentive remaining. Although it was not established for that purpose, the ITV Levy, and the fact that overseas programme sales income is exempt from it, has encouraged overseas co-financing by some ITV companies. The Levy arrangement is now under review by a government Working Party. In Australia there has been a boom in film and television production as a result of tax legislation giving investors a very considerable tax write-off, but this tax relief is only available to productions which are 100 per cent Australian in content. Canada and Germany both have government funds available subject to strict criteria which were established to encourage indigenous production.

Finally, there is the possibility of programme exchange. This is largely an area for broadcasters, rather than producers, to explore, and certainly in Europe there are positive moves towards reciprocal agreements which are designed to protect European broadcasting from becoming totally dominated by programmes bought in from the USA.

Combinations of various forms of co-financing can produce very complicated agreements, and, as the market widens through increased home video penetration, cable, satellite, etc., the scope for entrepreneurs is considerable. The broadcasting institutions have not yet, however, exhibited the same vigour or expertise as some independents in pursuing co-finance. Perhaps this is because they are preoccupied with running huge production centres and the flexibility and dealing skills required are not compatible with the bureaucratic attitudes and long-term planning of such organisations.

The packaging and broking of international productions is increasingly specialised and calls for many more attributes than a creative television producer is traditionally expected to possess. On the other hand, the opportunities for varied and challenging production are considerable and this is likely to encourage more producers to leave the shelter of institutions in favour of independent production. Just as the feature film industry supports packagers, agents, lawyers, tax specialists, etc., so will the independent television sector; indeed, in the USA it already does.

Whether or not this climate will produce a range of good programming or simply more formula market fodder depends on how the broadcasting networks develop. International co-financing is unlikely to be conducive to producing programmes which reflect a national culture, but as an audience we should welcome the opportunity to be exposed to other cultures. There will always be good programmes and bad ones and many mediocre ones. Sometimes co-financing degenerates into deal-making for its own sake, just as in-house production can mean no more than humdrum slot filling. There is, however, no reason why co-financing should produce programmes that serve the public less well than programmes wholly funded by one institution. Co-financing programmes do, after all, take considerably more effort and time to mount and are a cumbersome and erratic way of simply making money. Consequently they will continue to attract producers whose primary interest lies in making programmes.

Margaret Matheson

Co-production and co-finance are growing areas, areas to which some political importance is attached. They have obvious implications for public service broadcasting, for national broadcasting and for the idea of a national culture as represented in broadcasting.

ITV has benefited enormously from the financial strength of the ITV system which has enabled directors of programmes, or even heads of departments, to take programme decisions by themselves, without having to go around the world seeking agreement that such and such a series should be made.

On the run-up to Channel 4, I was asked whether the Channel's funds would be lavish enough to enable us to be so single-minded in deciding what programmes to make or commission and, if they were not, what degree of compromise did I envisage. I used to have qualms about the whole idea of co-production, because it seemed necessary that the production of television ought to have a consistent vision behind it, and that this was not likely to be the product of a committee or of the kind of compromise that might be involved in reaching an agreement between co-financing partners. As soon as the financial position of Channel 4 was clear, however, one could see that compromises would be necessary, although we would of course do our damnedest to protect the integrity of the work.

For this reason, and because I did not want Channel 4 to be an insular station, I bought *The Charterhouse of Parma*. I had seen some photographs; it looked splendid. Though I do not suppose I knew it at the time, it was produced in Germany and was funded by FR3 and RAI. Channel 4 had nothing whatsoever to do with it, except that we agreed to buy a UK licence. Perhaps I had hoped we were buying a masterpiece of European culture, and it was certainly very beautifully photographed. I soon discovered, however, one of the drawbacks to co-productions of this kind. Continental film-makers get extraordinary things on camera, but do not bother much about dialogue on location since they are going to dub whatever it is they film. It is not a case of shooting it in one language and dubbing it into another. They shoot, and then dub into a variety of languages. You can choose what language you would like it in. For *The Charterhouse of Parma* we had a choice of having it in French or Italian, or having it dubbed into English.

This is the kind of international co-operation, or 'Euro-pudding' as I have christened it, which I want as little to do with as possible. The Europeans do not feel the same way and maintain that it is a good idea.

Another example of the disadvantages of co-production is illustrated by what a colleague of mine said about a forth-coming Channel 4 programme: 'two of the performances were marvellous, the third, not a Britsh actor, was not as good as I would have wished it to be. I suppose that was the price we had to pay for engaging in co-production.'

Yet in spite of certain drawbacks, various forms of co-production are worth pursuing. For the year to the end of March 1985, set along side a total expenditure of £95 million, programmes to the value of £23 million depended on co-production financing. Channel 4's contribution was £11 million. In other words, our £11 million brought in another £12 million to the funding of those other programmes.

Of the twelve programmes involving co-production finance, in two there was joint editorial control between Channel 4 and a partner, and in seven Channel 4 had total editorial approval (though Channel 4 chooses to exercise this 'control' in a less formal way than other broadcasters). In another , a film directed by Bill Douglas, he, as Director, will have *editorial* control of the film; although we formally have approval at every stage given that it is going to cost £2.25 million. It is proper that he should have control, since the reason behind Channel 4's commitment was a desire to put *his* work on the screen.

Although it cannot strictly be described as a co-production, *La Piovra* is an example of another kind of co-finance agreement. It is an Italian drama, made in Italian principally for an Italian audience. We were content to leave control wholly in another country; nevertheless RAI were grateful to have some commitment from us to buy it before they made it.

On a more general level, co-production is thought to offer other than financial advantages. At the EBU General Assembly, held in Stockholm in June 1984, European broadcasters perceived public service broadcasting in Europe as under threat. Instead of being in control of their own broadcasting destinies, Europe is to be subjected to a proliferation of media outside the control of the public service broadcasters who run broadcasting in Europe. The EBU cited the grip and impact of cable and of satellite broadcasting. It saw the audience fragmenting, and also agglomerating and aggregating as satellites aim their signals not just at a national audience within the bounds of a national state responding to a national culture, but across national borders. In an attempt to combat this threat, the EBU approved a recommendation that it should start bringing people together to make programmes and it should do so formally as a broadcasting body. A special effort was required in the area of productions. Big organisations, big countries would want to continue to act independently, but small and medium-sized organisations would need assistance from other broadcasters. Since the monopoly of production and distribution which public service organisations had enjoyed was over, increased co-operation in the field of programmes was indispensable.

European governments are also beginning to address this question, and, in particular, to consider what should be done if, by satellite, a great many more American programmes are available to viewers than previously. Whether their concern arises from a desire to protect their national culture or from the extension of the role of public service national broadcasting in a technologically different era (or is simply a response to pressure from programme makers), several European governments want to spend EEC money on funding European television productions. Faced with a vastly increasing amount of material from the USA, their specific aim is to increase the proportion of work made in Europe and to be shown on European television screens.

The UK government is not in favour of spending funds on this, but would be perfectly happy for broadcasting organisations to spend their own money, or to raise private money. Channel 4 has decided to see if co-operation with European broadcasters is possible, to what extent it is desirable to increase it, and on what terms. We are not, however, prepared to commit ourselves to spending money regardless of whether there is a subject we actually want to do. For example, there are people both in broadcasting and in government who, in answer to the threat of an increased volume of American programmes and the dominant role which certain American programmes already play in the television culture, want to make a European *Dallas*. But a European *Dallas* would be a European Christmas cake and we should avoid it at all costs.

The BBC feels differently. It is going to put money into something called *Impact*; partly, no doubt, because by doing so it can say that it is helping British independent productions. Ten years ago the BBC had a soap opera called *Compact*. But *Impact*, which is to be produced in London, Paris and Hamburg, will be an even glossier 'magazine'. It is hard to understand why, considering all that is available, the BBC chooses to fund this project.

Although our public service broadcasting need not be essentially British, I believe the question of national culture is involved in the total output of public service television channels. We need a television on which the great issues which affect society can be debated. We also need a television whose fictions say something to that particular society about its own concerns, about its past and present and possible futures; and in its own accent, its own experience and its own humour. In other words we need work as good as *The Boys From the Blackstuff*. If the costs of television drama continue to rise, and if people want material of that quality and of that particularity to them, then it is a matter of public concern that this sort of work should be funded.

We do not want to live behind a wall marked: 'Foreigners keep out'. What I would passionately like to see in European broadcasting is an exchange of each other's best work rather than a collaboration on work which, because of the compromises involved in collaboration, may not do justice to the real needs of any of the countries participating.

Jeremy Isaacs

Jeremy Isaacs and Margaret Matheson speak as practitioners about the various forms of co-operation available to international production – co-production, co-financing, pre-sale, etc. Their accounts offer very useful documentation on current practice, and at the same time indicate some of the problems – both practical and cultural – which the increasing emphasis on the international television market poses for producers and programmers. This postscript, written from outside the practice of broadcasting, is intended simply to re-focus some of the issues which were raised in discussion at the seminar, and to add some questions of my own.

It is clear from the presentations, and it was reinforced by discussion, that the questions surrounding co-production are central to any debate about the future of British public service broadcasting. In many ways, by focusing public debate on whether or not the BBC should take advertising, the remit given to the Peacock Committee has effectively pre-empted a much wider consideration of the nature of public service in 'post-classical' broadcasting. Only if public service is taken to be co-extensive with the BBC, as 'classically' it was, is the question of advertising the only one to be addressed. If, on the other hand, public service broadcasting is seen as part of the ecology of national culture (or, more accurately, of national cultures), then the importance of the relationship between national production and international co-production becomes much clearer.

In fact, the difficulty of much of this discussion seems to me to lie precisely in the need to separate public service broadcasting from its 'classical' phase; from the phase in the forties when the BBC could speak of its 'cultural mission', of 'improving public taste', or when the BBC could be charged by a Labour Education Minister with the task of turning Britain into a 'Third Programme nation'. It also seems to me to lie in separating it from the somewhat hysterical defence which was mounted against the threat of commercial television in the 1950s. The record of Channel 4 demonstrates that there is no radical incompatibility between commerce and the service of the public. It is this system of associations which the history of public service invites which gives the arguments for de-regulation their force. Public service has a hard time living down its Reithian past, and to defend it means reconstituting some of its terms. It certainly means, in an age of new technologies and an international market, that the defence of public service broadcasting involves something more than protecting the BBC from advertising. In the most positive way, it means defining the relationship of television to a national culture or national cultures: culture conceived not simply as refinement, nor even simply as reflection, but as the representations by which people recognise themselves in their diversity, and even in their quite material and specific contradictions. It is here, in a very obvious way, that the question of national culture and international co-production rears its head.

In it most strident form, the question would be one of compatibility: are the requirements of the international market compatible with the interests of the national public which public service broadcasting is there to serve? Is co-production simply an instance of free enterprise seeking its most profitable, or at least its most cost-effective, market; and defining the public interest accordingly? (Can a public service be a free enterprise?) But at a more cautious, and probably more realistic level, the question is likely to be one of negotiated coexistence: what are the effects of a mixed economy of broadcasting in which domestic production (the service end of broadcasting) coexists with high-cost international co-productions (the prestige end)? Does co-production simply supplement existing domestic production, or does it, by introducing a new scale of professional values, begin to change the nature and aspirations of national broadcasting?

These are, rather obviously, not neutral questions. At the same time, while they are, I suppose, intended to ring some alarms, they are not intended as Cassandra-like predictions of the end of public service as we know it. The shift is not an apocalyptic one, and is not clarified by over-dramatisation. Clearly, the scope for co-production is limited, and, in that sense, it will always coexist with purely domestic production. My concern is, though, that the particular areas of television which are most likely to attract international co-financing are precisely those areas which have, in the recent past, been the cutting edge of television. In terms of a national culture, television drama has not simply reflected the nation, but has opened a space in which social discourse could be extended, lost histories could be retrieved, the comfortable images could be shaken. The space was not always filled, but it seems important that it was there. Is it still there, and will it survive the prestige of co-production?

Margaret Matheson indicates the limitations which co-financing imposes on the choice of subject: 'The subject is likely to be predictable and safe. . .'. Added to the negative temptation to self-censor subjects which are too localised, must be the positive temptation to seek out the marketable image. (I am writing from the perspective of Scotland, which has a long tradition of defining itself in terms of marketable images.) I am simply not sure that the artistic merit, the quality and the production values which can be achieved through the kind of funding which is available from international co-financing are an adequate compensation for safe subjects and marketable images.

It would clearly be absurd to call for an end to co-productions and a return to the simple values of public service. There is no way back to the national purity of the black-and-white Golden Age. Clearly, also, as both Jeremy Isaacs and Margaret Matheson indicated, new technologies and new production practices open real possiblities for an engagement with national cultures (which, one assumes, could be extended beyond the developed nations). The question then, in the end, is not one of resisting an international public service, but of securing the position of national public service systems and national cultures within that. It is at this level that issues of funding and culture cannot be separated. If public service is to be defended as a practical ideal rather than as merely a British tradition, it certainly has to be defended with funding as well as with public debate. But at a very practical level, it seems more sensible to me to mount the defence of public service against the arguments of de-regulation and the logic of the market on the grounds of a necessary engagement with the diversity and difficulty of national culture and national cultures, rather than on the nebulous and uncertain grounds of programme standards and artistic quality, Talking about money only *seems* more practical than talking about culture.

John Caughie

Broadcasting: national pasts and international futures

In his opening chapter Anthony Smith said that it was crucial to the personality of Channel 4 that it has 'developed strands of expression, has sought out the unexpressed, has stimulated not just half suppressed communities, but has given them the confidence to use the medium of television as if it were theirs'. I do not want to deny that claim but I do want to suggest that it is over-optimistic both about Channel 4's activities and indeed about the endeavour itself. It can too easily be read within a Romantic conception whereby an already constituted entity (the self or a particular community) simply 'expresses' its essential identity. In fact, however, we always express ourselves *to* someone and the addressee, the audience, is a crucial factor in what gets expressed (I talk differently to a child, a friend, a professional colleague, etc.) but also to the identity that is thus expressed. We are constructed by, amongst other things, our interlocutors. Expression is always related to an audience.

It is in terms of consideration of audience, and independently of any particular technical questions, that I want to talk about the central issues for public service broadcasting. In so doing I am going to eschew the seduction of the contemporary which are so much a feature of both the form and content of television. It is all too easy if one is caught up in the important and self-important world of broadcasting to become obsessed not only with this year but this month or even this week. This is enhanced by a tendency to think of broadcasting as something essentially, even quintessentially, modern; as something irrevocably bound up with the technical advances of the twentieth century. The word *broadcast* is taken from traditional farming and was used to describe the action by which a peasant threw seed in a wide arc over the land he was cultivating. It might appear that to move from that broadcasting to our scattering of electronic impulses is to move between incommensurable worlds. If, however, we think of broadcasting as the symbolic use of sound and image, and ignore its technical aspects then it is as old as the human species itself. Our medieval peasant had two official images: one provided by the cross in church and one by the king's head on the coins he all too infrequently saw. To these were added a soundtrack composed either of Latin in church or Norman French in the courts. Thus described, medieval television does not sound as though it would top today's ratings. These images and their incomprehensible voice-overs were nonetheless ideologically crucial to the various kinds of feudal tenure by which the aristocracy appropriated surplus production from the peasantry. There was, of course, resistance to the extraction of surplus, but it did not manifest itself solely in the sporadic and doomed peasants' revolt and *jacqueries* which punctuate the histories of medieval England and France. More important are the continuous traditions of unofficial broadcasting. The most striking of those in our contemporary folk memory are the sounds and images associated with witchcraft, but witchcraft is merely one of a range of unofficial symbolic practices which coexisted with the medieval Church. These would vary from locality to locality and would often provide more important communal identifications than that associated with the feudal monarchy.

From this perspective the history of the Reformation in England from Henry VIII to the Glorious Revolution of 1688 is best understood as the struggle to replace a broadcasting system using a foreign tongue and with a Roman director-general by one with an English soundtrack securely controlled by the City of London. If this extraordinary cultural revolution did break the privileged hold of a separately constituted Church over the national symbolic systems in which a society found its images of itself, it did not invite every member of the national community to participate in the production of these new national programmes. Reception was made obligatory through the recusancy and dissenting laws but broadcasting was limited to the Anglican orthodox. The unofficial, symbolic practices which had been tolerated by the medieval Church became the object of vigorous and constant attack, as is documented in Keith Thomas's *Religion and the Decline of Magic*. Those who were deprived of their local systems were not necessarily encouraged to enter the national Church as full participants. Almost all of the political struggles in England from 1588 to 1688 are largely struggles over who was to control this national Church and the social reproduction of the national culture which it embodied. Indeed, those struggles came to an end at the moment at which it is clearly possible to distinguish a national culture from a national Church, which then becomes merely a part (and an increasingly small part) of that culture. The struggles over these means of representation, which are always means of self-representation, continue. From an optimistic perspective, one can recount the history of Britain since the Reformation (and the West in general) as the witnessing of the increasing participation of ever larger groupings of people in the means of representation and self-representation. Raymond Williams has described this process as a 'Long Revolution' in which each technological advance accompanies a new era of political and cultural conflict. These conflicts involve struggles over education and the right of access to the technologies which produce symbolic systems as well as disputes over censorship and the forms of distribution which finally control the products of these symbolic systems. If we choose to regard long-term developments in the West since the seventeenth century from the perspective of the 'Long Revolution', we must add one very important reservation – that we are talking of the history of the West which has as the counterpoint to even its most optimistic notes the disenfranchising and elimination of other cultures.

Before returning to these international aspects, I want to consider the relations between broadcasting and the national culture the Reformation did so much to define, and which probably reached their apogee with the establishment of the BBC. The Reithian national church, so ably characterised by Anthony Smith in his opening lecture, was able to define the national community in probably its most extended form. By providing this extended national audience, Reith's BBC helped to constitute that sense of national identity which is identified with the Second World War. It would be idle to pretend that this national identity is a fiction, or to ignore the political, geographical and linguistic realities which underpin it; however, national identity tends to make or exclude the way in which an individual is a member of many communalities, often in contradiction with each other. Identities of class, race and gender cut across the identity afforded by citizenship of the nation. From the seventeenth century on, those identities have been effaced within the national culture and the early BBC might in certain ways be seen as the culmination of that effacement. Since the War, however, one of the most striking features of the national culture is the way in which these competing and contradictory collectivities have begun to assert themselves. In considering the proliferation of subcultures and the self-conscious organised resistance to the dominant national culture, it is usual to focus either on youth or the conflicts of class or sex. My own conviction is that, important as these are, the most significant development within our culture is that it has become multi-racial. More than anything else, this has been the crucial factor in a dynamic which has broken open the national mould in which the individual was held to be socially constituted. These developments are often described in terms of 'fragmentation', but such an account, with its implicit appeal to a unity before or beyond the fragments, ignores the way in which that unified national culture imposed itself by force and exclusion. The unfolding of that unity into diversity allows a much greater range of messages to find a voice. But if this diversity is to be fully explored through the medium of television, it may be that the national form itself must be broken. The process that I have been describing cannot be understood in terms of identifying communities within the nation and then simply allowing them to broadcast – for the finding of an audience may be the major way in which a community will constitute itself. It is in terms of the dialectic of recognition and identity that we find the constant anger of those communities which feel they have been denied access to the media; denied that possibility of finding a national audience which would confirm a political identity. For this anger to be felt, the community must already have largely constituted and confirmed its own identities. My argument is that television should be a major form for discovering and exploring communality. Here the national audience is the problem not the solution. Channel 4, and to a lesser extent, BBC2 before it, have attempted to address minority audiences, but, once again, in so far as those audiences are themselves already defined in terms of special interests, running from racial minorities to anglers and jazz *aficionados*, then television is simply being used to confirm existing divisions and identities.

The technology now exists for the combination of sound and image to be used in much more active relationships. The costs and technical complications which once made in-house production an absolute necessity are fast being superseded, and it is up to the broadcasting institutions to recognise this fact. Channel 4 does so in some sense, but its recognition of independent production is above all a recognition of those, who having been trained within them, wished to leave the large, bureaucratic, broadcasting institutions. There are gestures towards a more radical version of independent production in the workshops, but, important as this initiative is, it remains marginalised within the margins that Channel 4 itself constitutes. To develop fully the potential of an image-making policy would need a much greater transformation of the broadcasting system that has hitherto been envisaged: a huge editing structure which would involve both funding and programming.

Such a vision may seem as far from the present as the medieval peasant from the world of technology. Two questions can, however, be posed in relation to such a world of broadcasting.

The first is, who would control this massive spender of funds and allocator of air time? If we agree, as I am sure we do, that this is not an appropriate function for the executive arm of the State, then we are left with a problem. All the current forms of the control of broadcasting model themselves on the principles expressed in the selection of the governors of the BBC. The governors are not representatives but they are held to 'represent' a variety of interests in the national community. The problem is that the view of the national community that they embody is frozen *c.* 1922. (The particular iniquities of the current governors are beside this fundamental point.) Solutions, like those of the West German State, which attempt to produce an homology between control of the legislature and control of transmission, are equally immune to any developments within civil society which have not yet found *political* expression within the dominant institutions. I am not joking when I say that governors chosen at random, or an electoral college for governors chosen at random, would effectively constitute a much more serious bulwark against the domination of the *déjà-vu* of the political establishment.

At this point the second important question poses itself. Why consider the national level at all? If we are dealing in Utopias, why not allow a simple free-for-all of communication? The answer is, of course, scarcity. Scarcity of resources to produce programmes, scarcity of wave-lengths to transmit them and scarcity of arenas of political effectiveness. The nation, in many important senses, remains the single most effective instance for political action. As such it continues to be a critical arena of political and ideological struggle, and it demands national networks. One crucial feature of these national networks is to insist on heterogeneity from the other side. If we are to accept the multiplicity of communality, then it is idle to support cultural ghettos of uniformity. One of the great heritages of the BBC, one which outlasts its character as a national church, is its insistence on combining the forms of traditional high culture with forms of a more popular culture. In the drive to allow for more heterogeneity, it would be folly to discard those elements of the system which already encourage it. If our broadcasting systems should be flexible enough to allow new social identities to be recognised as new audiences are found, these social identities should then feed back to the national audience. The current defence of broadcasting pluralism is in terms of already defined national and minority audiences which the broadcasters, a separate category, address. I am advocating a more radical pluralism that would envisage the national audience as continuously transforming itself in a dialectic whereby minority audiences would constantly be developing and defining themselves but, once defined, would broadcast their definitions back to the wider community. It is a condition of such a vision that there is no separate category of broadcasters. We would become a nation of independent producers.

If it were possible to confine ourselves to the national level then what I have said, brief as it is, might well constitute a satisfactory programme for the future. The nation is not, however, simply under seige from within. In the seventeenth century capitalism and technology went hand in hand to constitute national cultures in Europe in a dialectical movement that reached from the printing press to the workshop, via the relays of schools, bureaucracies and national armies. In the twentieth century the advances in electronic technology and the possibilities for the accumulation of wealth go hand in hand across the networks of research institutes and international television (and mutually assured destruction) to construct an international culture of apocalyptic powers. There is a powerful argument to the effect that the economies of the current technologies assure American dominance of the international medium of television. The vast resources of revenue made available by American audiences mean that America is always able to sell its cultural products abroad for a fraction of their cost of production. They are, therefore, much cheaper than the comparable home product. In addition, the very production values which make American programmes so 'watchable' are often beyond the scale that smaller national audiences could justify.

One possible response to the international dominance of American television would be to combat it at the level of the national; to reassert a national identity against this foreign invasion. Whatever the legitimacy of such a response for Third World countries, it seems to me that in the context of Britain such a response can only be regressive; a return to the most repressive features of nationalism.

Two other responses do, however, suggest themselves. The first is at the level of national broadcasting systems. On 1 January 1973, in honour of our adhesion to the European Economic Community, BBC1 broadcast a full day of programmes from the member nations of the community. I don't know what the viewing figures were but I would hazard an educated guess that they did not inspire any BBC executive to repeat the experiment. If there had been any serious political desire to turn the Community into a collectivity, then the question of European television would be at the top of every political and cultural agenda. If it were, then the problems of language would have to be confronted at a more radical level than any broadcasting or educational institution has dreamed of to date. The extent of the problem can be gauged anecdotally by considering Godard's film, *Le Mepris,* made in the early sixties. Set in Rome's *Cinecittà* it uses a co-production of a film for its plot. The differing languages of the protagonists require a translator, an Italian girl, who interprets from one language to another. When the film was released in Italy it was dubbed. At this point the translator's lines lost all validity and, in desperation, the Italian distributors invented lines and a role in the plot for her. Godard's reaction – to enjoin all Italian cinema-lovers to blow up the cinemas where a soundtrack had been thus violated – was characteristically excessive, but was nonetheless characteristically acute. The difficulties of constructing a genuine European level of broadcasting are enormous.

It may even be a delusion to consider such a European strategy, since it would ignore two facts. First, at the economic level, while it might compete with America, it would simply compete for domination of world markets. Second, and more important, it would accept the aesthetic argument that the immense popularity of American television and the immense popularity of American film that accompanied and preceded it can be explained away in terms of economic dominance of the technology. Such an argument is infused with deeply anti-democratic conviction. The popular taste which accepts and applauds the products of American mass culture is held to be automatically deficient. There is every reason to distrust such automatic cultural reflexes. If we take the example of popular music we can recall that the whole development which joined an electronic technology to black musical forms in America in the 1950s was viewed by the European Left as cultural imperialism of the most pernicious variety. Yet it is that music which has consistently provided European youth with the most important form with which to articulate their desires and revolts. The technology of rock music, however, has allowed many to appropriate these sounds and play them back with fresh inflections and emphases. What is distressing about the tele-visual and filmic forms is that they seem to preclude the possibility of feedback, the ability of spectators to edit-in their reflections, to register their differences from, as well as their similarities to, the figures of American popular culture. This editing is, of course, undertaken everywhere – in dress, in mannerisms, in the phenomenon of fashion as it manifests itself variously from Third World shanty towns to First World suburbs – but it is important that this registering of difference should be able to use the same medium as the original message.

Here the necessity to engage with the international fea-tures of television rejoins the necessity to break with the prevailing national mould and to produce an image-making as well as an image-receiving society. Between the home movie and the Hollywood epic the new technologies offer a multitude of intermediate stages. The task now is to ensure that these technologies do not subordinate all these levels to the simple international dominance of Sky Channel and its few international competitors. Public service must be inter-preted as the commitment to provide structures of broadcast-ing that will allow the widest range of audiences. The aim must be to allow as many producers as possible to find *their* audience.

This chapter has been deliberately Utopian and unspecific. It has sought to provide an historical over-view and some long term aims. The difficulties are, however, immense and should not be minimised. The history of community and access television, both inspired by something of the perspec-tives collaborated here, has been dismal. The importance of professionalism and production values are easily minimised on paper. Audiences are not so easily convinced. However, as we enter a new era of technological advance, it is important to restate priorities. These priorities have the enormous advantage of providing a set of cultural objectives in the West which do not, in their very essentials, entail the subjugation of non-Western cultures.